Christ

Christ for all Seasons

Meditations for Lent, Easter and Christmas

by

Thomas à Kempis

(edited by Peter Toon)

Marshall Pickering

for

Lorna Khoo
Geoffrey Abisheganaden
Carl-Gunnar Lundgren

to recall happy times in
Singapore, August 1988

Marshall Morgan and Scott
Marshall Pickering
34–42 Cleveland Street, London W1P 5FB. U.K.

British Library CIP Data

Thomas à Kempis, 1379 or 80–1470
Christ for all seasons
1. Christian life—Devotional works
I. Title II. Toon, Peter
242

ISBN 0-551-01785-6

Text set in Baskerville by Avocet Robinson, Buckingham
Printed in Great Britain by Anchor Press Ltd, Colchester, Essex

Contents

Introduction

LENT

EASTER

CHRISTMAS

Introduction

Thomas à Kempis is best known for his *Imitation of Christ* (1418). This classic has been translated into at least ninety-seven languages and has been through at least three thousand editions. In contrast his *Meditations on the Life of Christ*, originally written in Latin, has only been translated into a few Western European languages and has gone through fifty or so editions. However, the *Meditations* holds an important key to the right understanding of the *Imitation*. For there is no imitation of Christ except first through meditating upon him, his person and his word.

From his own experience as a Brother of the Common Life in the community at Windesheim, as well as through learning from the traditions of spirituality coming from St Bernard of Clairvaux and St Francis of Assisi, Thomas à Kempis had clear ideas as to how believers are to imitate (truly follow) Jesus. It was all a matter of rightly receiving the grace of God given in Jesus Christ by the Holy Spirit in various divinely-appointed ways and means. And it involved the practice of definite disciplines to fulfil the teaching of St Paul who wrote: 'Continue to work out your salvation with fear and trembling, for it is God who works in you to will and do what pleases him' (Phil. 2:12-13).

The discipline which gives meaning and purpose to the rest is meditating upon the Four Gospels in order thereby to encounter the living Lord Jesus. Here are the opening lines of the *Imitation* which state this intention:

> 'He that followeth me shall not walk in darkness', saith the Lord. These are the words of Christ (John 8:12) by which we are reminded that we must copy his life and conduct, if we wish to be truly enlightened and to be delivered from all blindness of heart. To meditate on the life of Jesus should, therefore, be our chief study.

Imitation is primarily of the virtues and attitudes of the risen Christ rather than of his particular way of life, diet and clothing in ancient Galilee (1 Cor. 11:1).

But what did Thomas mean by meditation? To arrive at the answer we must recognize that there is a vast difference between meditation as practised in the East by Hindus and Buddhists and meditation as practised in the West in traditional Catholic and Protestant communities. Practitioners of Eastern methods commonly deny that meditation ever includes 'thinking about something'. In contrast, classic Christian meditation always begins (but never ends) with thinking about something – namely the revealed Word of God. Thomas à Kempis was very definitely in the Western, Christian tradition for his meditation involved thinking about the living Lord Jesus as he is portrayed in the four Gospels.

More precisely, meditation for Thomas à Kempis involved the following aspects: (a) carefully and prayerfully reading a portion of a Gospel; (b) using his reason to understand it and his imagination to picture the scene as understood; (c) imaginatively placing himself in that scene so that he became a participant and was able to watch and hear Jesus at first hand; and (d) having felt the power of Jesus and heard his authoritative word, resolving to imitate his attitude and virtues, and then engaging in prayer to God the Father in the name of Jesus. He practised such meditation each day for a substantial period of time – up to one hour.

This form of meditation is particularly suited to meditation upon the contents of the Gospels: meditation upon the Epistles demands a greater use of consideration and reflective thought (see futher P. Toon, *Meditating upon God's Word*, Darton, Longman & Todd, London, 1988).

The effect of such meditation upon the Gospels (when accompanied, of course, by other necessary Christian disciplines such as the cultivation of simplicity, submission and service and the participation in Christian worship and fellowship) is to renew in the soul the true image of God (Gen. 1:26-27) after the pattern of Christ, who is the true image of the invisible God (Rom. 8:29; 1 Cor. 11:7; 15:49; Col. 1:15; 3:10). To use an illustration – the effect of genuine meditation upon the Gospels is like the painting each day of a very fine film of paint upon the surface of a building. Over a long period of time a substantial coat of paint is created. Likewise, over a long period of time the soul – mind, heart and will – is (we may say) thoroughly imbued with the spirit of Christ.

We all recognize that meditation of this kind does not come easily. Not only must we make the space and time (be it only twenty minutes a day), we must also both conquer wandering thoughts and break down inner resistance to the call and demand of Jesus. Anyone coming to this kind of meditation today cannot expect results immediately. He or she must resolve to stick with it not merely for weeks but for months before its real spiritual benefits will be felt.

Thomas à Kempis practised for years and knew the ups and downs as well as the problems and blessings. The careful reader of the *Imitation*, in pondering its rich supply of maxims and apothegms, will gradually become aware of this. However, even a man of the spiritual depth of Thomas cannot convey in words the total experience of an act of meditation upon a part of a Gospel. Therefore, we should not expect too much from his written *Meditations*. Rather, we should approach them looking for indications of the movement of the reason, imagination, feelings and will as they are encountered by Christ through the scriptural text. What the *Meditations* can do is to help the beginner and the busy person to gain insights into biblical meditation which no textbook, however well written, can supply. The proof of the pudding, it is said, is in the eating: the proof that Thomas' *Meditations* can inspire and help will come to those who conscientiously use them.

Before explaining the format of this book and the choice of meditations, it is perhaps necessary to offer several explanatory comments which hopefully will make the reading more productive. First of all, Thomas believed that the four Gospels were written by apostolic men as they were inspired and guided by the Holy Spirit. In the second place, he believed that the Scriptures were written primarily for the people of God to make them holy and obedient, trustful and humble, loving and joyful before the Lord. Thirdly, he believed that Jesus is alive in heaven and through the Holy Spirit (= the Spirit of Christ) is present in God's Church, in the sacraments and in the sacred page of the Bible. Therefore, he approached the scriptural text expecting it to become the door through which Christ came forth to meet him.

Finally, we need to be clear that the theme of imitating Christ does not remove – indeed it complements – the theme of Christ's substitutionary and expiatory atonement. Thomas would have agreed with St Bernard who wrote:

Three principal things I perceive in this work of our salvation: the pattern of humility, in which God emptied himself; the measure of love, which he stretched even unto death, and that the death of the cross; the mystery of redemption in which he bore that death which he underwent. The two former of these without the last are as if you were to paint on the air. A very great and most necessary example of humility, a great example of charity and one worthy of all acceptation he has set us; but they have no foundation, and, therefore, no stability, if redemption be wanting. I wish to follow with my strength the lowly Jesus; I wish him who loved me and gave himself for me to embrace me with the arms of his love, which suffered in my stead; but I must also feed on the Paschal Lamb, for unless I eat his flesh and drink his blood I have no life in me. It is one thing to follow Jesus, another to hold him, another to feed on him – neither the example of humility, nor the proofs of charity are anything without the mystery [sacrament] of our redemption. (*Treatise against the Errors of Abelard*, ch. 9.)

Before there can be any imitation there must be redemption. And this Thomas made clear in the fourth part of his *Imitation of Christ* in his presentation of the receiving of Holy Communion. There is no reason why we should not also share the experience of Thomas, finding through meditation that Christ comes from the sacred page into our hearts and lives. As the *Imitation of Christ* has helped hundreds of thousands to follow Christ, we pray that these *Meditations* will help thousands more to use their Bible profitably and know the joy of communion with Christ through the discipline of meditation. Please read them slowly, thoughtfully and prayerfully.

All the meditations used in this book are translations made from *De Vita et Beneficiis Jesu Christi Salvatoris Nostri Meditationes et Orationes* (critical edition by M. J. Pohl, Freiburg i. Br, 1902). We have used the translation of W. Duthoit,[1] checking it against that of A. Wright and S. Kettlewell.[2] However, in order to fit the meditations into a suitable scheme for Lent, Easter and Christmas, we have had to shorten some of the longer ones.

We suggest that you first of all read the scriptural passage slowly – and at least twice – before carefully reading the meditation by Thomas à Kempis. Hopefully, after using his meditations you will feel able to attempt similar meditations yourself on other parts of the four Gospels.

Trinity 1988   Peter and Vita Toon
                                                Staindrop Vicarage

Notes
1. *Prayers and Meditations on the Life of Christ* (Kegan, Paul, French, Trubner & Co. Ltd., London, 1904).
2. *Meditations on the Life of Christ* (Parker & Co. Ltd., Oxford and London, 1892).

Forty Meditations

for

Lent

Jesus is tested

Matt. 4:1-11; Luke 4:1-13

 bless you, and give thanks to you, O Lord Jesus Christ, for the holy fast, which, in the loneliness of the desert, you kept for forty days and forty nights, that you might be to us a model of holy abstinence.

I praise and magnify you, O Lord Jesus Christ, food of angels, and refreshment of men, for the many pangs of hunger, for the wondrous abstinence, for the stern chastisement of your most sacred body, for the many long watchings, for the holy prayers, and for the most pure meditations, which you accomplished there in the wilderness.

I praise and magnify you for ever for your mighty conflict with the devil; for the many attacks of that most wicked tempter; for your scorning of all his evil suggestions; for the wise answers from Holy Scripture, with which you confounded him; and for your most glorious victory over the three cardinal sins – all which you mercifully brought to pass for the perpetual confounding of Satan, and for the strengthening of our weakness.

On meekly bended knees, I join the holy angels, who, with the reverence which is your due, then ministered to you, in praising and adoring you: and I beseech you that, so long as I live in the wilderness of this present world, you would give me daily bread, the help of your grace, comfort in tribulation, firmness under temptation, and protection against all the snares of the enemy.

I believe and confess that you are Christ, the Son of God, very God, and Lord of angels, Creator and Redeemer of the human race, in all points proved and tempted in the weakness of our flesh; so that you might be led to pity us; and having suffered, being tempted like as we are, might be able to cure us from the diseases of our sins.

O kind Jesus, most dauntless champion, who for my sake fasted so unflinchingly, and so bravely fought and conquered, help me, I beseech you, to fight manfully against the world, the flesh and the devil, and to repel with steadfast heart every assault of the evil one! **Amen**.

3

Judas betrays Jesus

Matt. 26: 14-16, 23-25

 bless you, and give thanks to you, O Lord Jesus Christ, of goodness supreme, of majesty eternal, for the wicked sale of you by your own disciple, by whom you were sold for so paltry and mean a price as thirty pieces of silver.

I praise and glorify you for the surpassing meekness of your forbearance with that treacherous disciple. Not only were you not moved to anger, or to the use of harsh words, against him, but also (although you knew the treachery which he was so soon to perpetrate) you did not at once make known his villainy to his fellow-disciples, nor suspend him from Holy Communion.

O most gentle Lord Jesus, how great is your patience, how great my impatience!

Woe is me that I find it so hard to bear with my brother, if anything is said or done to me which I do not like! You did for so long a time uncomplainingly bear with your disciple Judas, who was shortly to sell and betray you, whereas I, for some slight wrong, fly at once into a passion, and concoct all sorts of plans for revenging or excusing myself. At such a time what becomes of my meekness, and of my patience?

Help me, O good Jesus, I beseech you, and instil into my heart more and more fully the virtue of your gentleness; for without your special grace and guidance, I cannot have the blessing of quietness of soul amidst the worries and the troubles, of which in this life there are so many. **Amen**.

Jesus bears our sorrows

Matt. 26: 23-46

I bless you, and give thanks to you, O Lord Jesus Christ, Maker and Redeemer of all the faithful, for the sad beginning of your most bitter Passion; for the exceeding distress of your soul; for the anxiety and dread, which, in the weakness of your human nature (taken upon you of your own free will for our sakes) you felt.

As the hour of your betrayal drew near, you did begin to be fearful and very sad. Nor were you ashamed of confessing this sadness to your disciples, for you said: 'My soul is sorrowful even unto death.' O wondrous dispensation of God! You, the Lord of all power, who but a short while since had given strength to your disciples for the strife, now bear yourself as one who is weak, and wanting in strength and courage.

And all this you did undergo in order the more perfectly to comfort us in weakness and faintheartedness, lest perchance some one of us, when sorely tempted, should despair of pardon or salvation; for if such an one should feel himself less cheerful than he should be under suffering, less brave than he should be, in enduring trials of the flesh, he may still be able to say with you: 'Nevertheless not as I will, but as Thou wilt.'

O most loving Jesus, my only hope in every trouble and distress, make me, I pray you, to ponder with a heart full of compassion, the sorrowful beginning of this your blessed Passion; and from this sad prelude to go on by degrees to meditate upon the still more bitter parts of it, so that I may be able, from each several part, to gather for the wounds of my soul some healing medicine.

Grant that I may bear with patient courage, for the glory of your name, whatever troubles may be awaiting me; that I may never fall into despair, no matter how severe the tribulation may be, but may in all things resign myself to the good pleasure of your divine providence. **Amen.**

5

Jesus in anguish

Mark 14: 32-42; Luke 22: 42-46

bless you, and give thanks to you, O Lord Jesus Christ, stay of angels, refuge of the distressed, for your agonizing prayer, and your lowly falling flat upon the ground; when thrice, upon your bended knees, you earnestly and devoutly beseeched your heavenly Father that, if it were possible, the chalice of your Passion might pass from you; and yet you even added the words: 'Nevertheless not as I will, but as Thou wilt.'

I praise and glorify you, for your mighty struggle against the fear of death, and of the anguish of your most bitter Passion; when the flame of divine love burnt so fiercely within you, as to thrust out all human fear.

I praise you, and give thanks to you, for the copious shedding of your sweat of blood; when, being in agony, you prayed yet more fervently; and, against the order of nature, you gave out from your body, as sweat, drops of blood.

I adore you, and give you glory, for your humble acceptance of the angelic consolation, which you, the Maker and the King of the heavenly host, for the more strengthening of our feebleness, did not disdain to receive at the hands of angels: that so, weaklings we are, we may be led to seek, not the comfort which is but for a moment, but that true strength which comes from above.

O most sweet Jesus, with what fervour of love must you have loved me, that you prayed for me so earnestly as to give forth – in your great desire to suffer for me – in place of natural sweat, your own warm blood, trickling down upon the ground.

O almighty Creator of my soul, and perfect pattern of my life, I praise you, and magnify you for ever, for your boundless resignation; and for your complete conquest of your own will, and of all your feelings as a man, which would have made you shrink from pain and death. I praise and magnify you for having at once, without the least wavering, when the hour of your Passion was at hand, resigned yourself freely and willingly to your Father's will, saying: 'Father, not my will, but Thine, be done.' These were gracious words with which you magnified your Father's glory: and heaped further benefits upon us; and yet more firmly trod the devil under foot; and you showed forth, to those who believe in you, more plainly than ever before, the model of perfection, the ensign of salvation, and the path of the highest virtue.

O adorable Jesus, you whose example we must ever keep before us, grant, I most earnestly beseech you, that I may obtain the fruit of this thrice-repeated prayer, and that I may strive to imitate the example of your self-denial.

Give me grace manfully to bring into subjection to the spirit the stubbornness of my flesh; to crush all shrinking from bodily pain; to use prayer more often than before; to be ever watchful therein; to trust lovingly in you for help; to leave confidently in your hands the issue of all my undertakings; utterly to renounce my own will in everything; and to be always ready courageously to bear whatever troubles may come upon me. **Amen.**

Jesus meets his betrayer

Matt. 26: 47-56; John 18: 1-11

 bless you, and give thanks to you, O Lord Jesus Christ, our Saviour and Deliverer, for your cheerful readiness to suffer. When your most cruel enemies, and Judas, your most wicked betrayer, came, in the dead of night, with a great multitude, with swords and clubs, and torches and weapons, to take you, as if you had been a robber, you yourself went forth at once to meet them saying: 'Whom seek ye? I am he. If therefore you seek me, let these go their way.' At this first word of your power all their arrogant boldness was discomfited, and utterly put to confusion. For, as soon as you said this to them, they went backwards and fell to the ground. What then would have happened if, at your bidding, twelve legions of angels had come upon them?

But it was to suffer that you came into the world, and so, instead of using your divine power, you showed forth your most gracious forbearance. You made plain, by one short word, the majesty of your power: and now you allowed those impious men to have dominion over you, and to wreak their venomous spite against you for a season; so that you might make it plain that it was of your own free will that you were entering upon your Passion, and for the accomplishment of the work of our redemption, and for the fulfilment of the predictions of the Prophets of Israel.

I praise and glorify you, O Lord Jesus Christ, most innocent

8

Lamb of God, for your unspeakable gentleness, and for your invincible spirit of meekness, in that you were not inflamed with anger against your most wicked betrayer, and did not indignantly turn your back upon him. Instead, you entered into friendly conversation with him; and addressing him with your usual kindness, did suffer him, unworthy as he was, to kiss your most sweet lips, saying to him with those gentle words: 'Judas, dost thou betray the Son of Man with a kiss?' Alas, he who had been one of the company of your apostles, neither fearing you as his Judge, nor pitying you as his friend did not shrink from his most horrible villainy; instead, he put himself at the head of that band of evil men, gave them a sign saying, 'Whomsoever I shall kiss, that is he, hold him fast.' O vilest disciple of a master most loving! O servant most perfidious of a master most faithful!

O how wonderful was your love, how splendid was your patience, O most meek, most loving Jesus. Even at the time of your arrest and base betrayal, you did not forget your old friendship and tenderness! You repaid so great a wrong by a gift of healing. By the touch of your sacred hand you made whole again the ear of the High Priest's servant which Peter had cut off. And when he would have protected you from your assailants, you made him hold his hand, saying: 'Put up again thy sword into its place. The chalice which my Father hath given me, shall I not drink it? For thus it must be.'

Now, therefore, O my God I beseech you to give me, frail reed that I am, greater patience when things go wrong with me; and when my enemies insult me, or when charges are brought against me, of which I know myself to be innocent, let not sudden anger get the better of me, nor a love of revenge stir me up to render evil for evil. Grant me grace not to shrink from criticism but to take reproaches in good part, and to regard as a friend whoever blames or reproaches me the most. Give me grace not to feel angry at any harshness shown to me, and not to bear malice for any unjust complaint made against me; but to let the thought of your most gentle endurance of the wrongs done to you, strengthen me to rejoice in my own, and fill me with a desire to suffer even worse wrongs for love of you. **Amen**.

LENT 6

Jesus is taken captive

Mark 14: 43-52

bless you, and give thanks to you, O Lord Jesus Christ, hope of the saints, and their strong power in every distress, for the violent seizure of you by your hateful enemies; for the insolent laying upon you of the sacrilegious hands of those who sought to hold you; for the fierce looks they cast upon you; for the threatening shouts of the soldiers; for their rough and cruel binding of you; for their rude and ungentle holding of you fast; for their hasty and disorderly leading away of you; for the haste and the violence with which they dragged you along; when, with wild tumult, you were hurried away by vile and worthless scoundrels to your death; while the disciples, who were so dear to you, either fled, or with eyes full of grief and sorrow looked upon you from afar.

O King of kings, O Lord who rules over all your creatures, and alone among mortals are free, how could you bear to be thus violently seized by evil hands, and to be led away in such haste and disgrace, by men whom you had yourself created, and to whom you had always done good? Alas! how grievous was the crime committed against you, how audacious the insult to your sovereign Majesty, when you, the Deliverer of souls, were bound with a malefactor's cord; when you, who were altogether free from sin, were led away a prisoner, as if you had been the vilest of robbers! But you, my most loving Jesus, supreme author of all virtues, willed to endure all these things most patiently for our sakes, that you might set us an example of perfect meekness, and might fulfil that most plain of the prophecies of Isaiah: 'He shall be led as a sheep to the slaughter, and shall be dumb as a lamb before His shearer, and He shall not open His mouth. He was offered because it was His own will.'

Feel compassion, then, O my soul, for your most loving Lord God, an ill-used prisoner, enduring of his own free will all these things because of your sins. Groan deeply, and let your eyes be wet with tears of sorrow, at the thought of the only-begotten Son of God being treated with such indignity for your sake. See what those wicked Jews are doing. They hold Jesus captive, they lead him bound before Annas, and before Caiaphas the High Priest: but when he is seized he does not resist; when he is bound he does not complain; when he is led away he does not struggle with his captors; when he is being dragged along he utters no ill-word; but he goes meekly on, is quiet as a lamb, follows his captors as one who is guiltless, bears everything as one who is humility itself.

I pray you, then, O my God, that the thought of the bitterness of the grievous restraint thus put upon you may sink deep into my heart; may often rouse me, and chiefly when it is the time for daily prayer; may drive from me all listlessness; and may make me constant, active, and watchful, in praising you, so that I may at least make some return for your love, and for the hardships endured by you, who, for my sake, at night-time was born, and at night-time was betrayed, was seized, and was bound with cords. At night-time, therefore, O Lord, will I ever remember your holy name, calling to mind what great things you have suffered for me, the chief of sinners.

May your painful bonds win for me true liberty; may they hold me back from unprofitable wandering and by strong discipline keep me ever in your service. May I not find it hard to overcome and get rid of self-will. Stiff-necked and self-willed as I am by nature, may a disciplined life, and the subjection of my own inclinations be made to me my greatest happiness; and may I have grace to bring my own inner life, at least in some small measure, into conformity with the example which you have set, when you were bound, and held captive. **Amen**.

11

Jesus is forsaken

Matt. 26:56; Mark 14: 50-51

 bless you, and give thanks to you, O Lord Jesus Christ, good Shepherd and gracious Master, for your most sad abandonment and for your loneliness, in the extremity of your need; when you were left, by all your disciples and friends, quite alone in the midst of your most cruel enemies. For your brethren, and your familiar friends – who had promised to die, and to give their lives for you – when the need came, one and all forsook you, and fled.

I praise and glorify you, for that tenderness of heart, which caused you to suffer so cruelly from the cowardice with which your disciples turned their backs on you and deserted you, when leaving you their Shepherd in the midst of wolves, they were dispersed like sheep, every one to his own, even as you had foretold to them. Great indeed must have been the sadness, great indeed the anguish and the grief, which possessed the hearts of the disciples when they saw you, their Lord and Master, whom they had left all to follow, so violently torn from them, and hurried away to death.

But you, O Lord, to whom all things are known, and who does not allow anything to happen without its fulfilling some purpose of your own, did permit these chosen vessels to show such great weakness in order that out of it greater good might come. This was to lead them to know their own frailty, and to sympathize with that of other weak brethren; and so ever afterwards they remained more distrustful of themselves, more fervent in spirit, more humble and more devout.

How useful it is for me to meditate diligently upon this subject, and never to think too highly of myself. If the apostles of Christ gave way in time of tribulation, what is a most frail and unprofitable weakling likely to do, when even a slight temptation assails him? Some indeed, O Lord, would cry shame upon your holy apostles for their base desertion of you, and because, being beside themselves from fear, they tried to escape; but such men forget what an everyday thing it is for people to go astray under the stress of love or hate, as the case may be.

Do not, then, I pray you, my most dear Lord, let me fall a victim to so great spiritual madness, as ever to turn aside from any holy purpose which I have taken in hand; and grant me grace to follow you wherever you go be it to life or to death. May I never forsake you in time of adversity, nor be drawn away by my own lusts so as to fall into sin; but may I rather, for the love of you, and in pursuit of what is good, remain firm under straits and hardships, of whatever kind; lest, at any time, through my own fault, I should come to lose my highest good.

May I do everything reverently, humbly remembering my own weakness. May the fall of holy Peter, and the flight of the apostles, be no stumbling-block to me; but may these things rather be a warning against sin. May the restoration of your apostles to your favour, which followed upon their repentance, give me a strong hope of again obtaining mercy after a fall of my own – for there is no one so holy as never to fall into sin of some kind. And when it so happens that my friends and acquaintances turn away from me (or those whom I love well think evil of me, and treat me as one who is of no account, and as it were a stranger to them) then, O Lord, grant that I may, for my own comfort, keep in mind your most grievous desertion and rejection, and count it gain to be deprived of all human consolation – if only I may thereby, in my small degree, be conformed to what you had to undergo.
Amen

LENT 8

Annas arraigns Jesus

John 18: 12–14, 19–23

bless you, and give thanks to you, O Lord Jesus Christ, guide of our life, and author of our salvation, for your first indictment before Annas, the Priest, where you were questioned about many things, and in return for your meek and truthful answer, were rudely smitten on the cheek.

I praise and magnify you, my glorious King Jesus Christ, for the dishonour thus done to you, and for the shameful blow which you received from the hand of an insolent servant, when in return for your answer he gave you a heavy blow upon your face, saying: 'Answerest Thou the High Priest so?' And even after all this you did not fail, O most gentle Jesus, undisturbed in mind or speech, meekly to make answer to him again, saying: 'If I have spoken evil, give testimony of the evil; but if well, why smitest thou Me?'

O most vile and impious servant, how was it that you did not fear to strike the face of your Creator, deserving of all love, with your guilty hands! How unspeakable, my adorable Jesus, was the virtue of meekness which shone forth in you, when, instead of avenging so insulting a blow with immediate chastisement, you calmly expostulated with him who struck you!

Consider now, O Christian, and say whether, for love of Jesus, you could endure a slap in the face. You who cannot bear a hard word without losing your temper, how could you bear to be smitten on the mouth? You grieve over the uncalled-for violence offered to your Lord; but much more sad, surely, is it that you should be so little able to endure, for Christ's sake, even trivial wrongs. You make grand resolutions, your ideals are lofty; but the first reproachful word upsets you, and you find yourself weaker than you had thought yourself to be. Flee then to Jesus, and pray him more earnestly than ever before to give you the virtue of patience.

O good Jesus, strength and stay of the troubled soul, teach me to bear, with an even mind, blame and reproach; teach me, when complaints are unjustly made against me, not angrily to fight against them, but rather to get the better of them by meekly holding my peace; or, if speech be needed, may my words be such as to make of my adversaries friends. Put a right and loving word into my mouth in the presence of those that set themselves against me; and, when the hand of the wicked is lifted up against me, give me, O most gentle Jesus, for my impregnable shield, modest and imperturbable calmness of mind.

Forgive me, O most merciful Jesus, for having so often offended you; for having been so ready to go astray after that which has profited me nothing; for not having kept my heart steadfastly fixed upon that which I had resolved to do. Also, when I consider my ways, how often do I find that I waste my time upon vain things which can never profit, and fail, alas, in keeping your sacred Passion ever in my view! You have trodden the narrow way before me, and I pass by without a tear, as if your anguish were no concern of mine. Take pity, I pray you, upon my cold dull heart, and fill it with a loving remembrance of your most bitter Passion. **Amen**.

Peter denies Jesus

Matt. 26: 69-75; Luke 22: 61-62

 bless you, and give thanks to you, O Lord Jesus Christ, who know all things before they come to pass, for having warned your over-confident disciple Peter, by foretelling to him his fall.

I glorify you for the anguish of your soul at the grievous dishonour brought upon you by the thrice-repeated denial of you by Peter the apostle, when, to the challenge of a woman, he made answer in the words: 'I know not the man.'

I praise and magnify your name for ever, for that gentle look which you did mercifully vouchsafe to cast upon blessed Peter, so that, immediately upon the second crowing of the cock, he might be brought to a sense of his guilt; and going out at once from among those wicked men, might mourn with bitter tears, and with deep contrition of heart, his terrible sin of denying you.

He indeed did not, like wretched Judas, fall hopelessly into the pit of despair; but saved by your unspeakable mercy, and trusting to your boundless store of pity and loving-kindness, of which he had so often felt the tenderness, he sought at once, with bitter lamentations, that wholesome medicine of penance, which you have provided for the healing of the disease of sin; and he found set open wide before him the gate of infinite mercy.

O the surpassing love and pity of the Saviour! How inexhaustible is that fountain of divine mercy and overflowing grace, which has been opened to us; to which the sinner may always resort in the sure hope of being forgiven, and the righteous of always finding therein abundant stores of grace! Would to God, then, that I might always have ready such a fountain of tears, that, like blessed Peter, I might be sure of worthily bewailing my sins, and of obtaining the pardon which they need, and the grace which I have lost.

Peter, indeed, fell because, in fear of death, he thrice denied the truth; but I, on the slightest cause, daily swerve from the path of virtue, and in many things sin against eternal truth. Peter, when he fell, rose again at once: I, alas, fall more easily than he did, but my recovery is not so swift; seldom do I bewail my sins; careless is the watch I keep over myself; I shun not danger as I ought.

Peter shed bitter tears of repentance; taught by his fall he avoided occasions of sin; he sought for a secret place wherein to weep; and, by prayers full of holy grief, he washed away the stains which his careless words had brought upon his soul. How fruitful is the tear, which so soon blots out the sins we have committed, and by means of which even grace, which has been lost, may be recovered . . .

And now, with sighs, which come from the bottom of my heart, I beseech you, O most kind and merciful Lord Jesus, to turn upon me those loving eyes, with which you looked upon Peter after he had denied you, and to grant me speedily the grace of holy contrition, so that I may be cleansed from all the sins, whether deliberate or indeliberate, which I have committed against you.

Listen to the groans of my heart; heal the wounds of my evil conscience; give me once more the light of your grace; and keep from perishing a penitent soul, for the redemption of which you were content to endure such anguish, such insults, and in the end the cruel death of the Cross.   **Amen.**

Jesus is taken to Caiaphas

John 18: 12-14, 24; Matt. 26: 57-68

 bless you, and give thanks to you, O Lord Jesus Christ, perpetual High Priest, for being so contemptuously led away from the house of Annas to that of Caiaphas the high priest, where the Scribes and Elders were gathered together to take cruel counsel against you. Ah! with what unholy joy were they filled, when they saw you whom they had long wished to seize – but could not, because your hour was not yet come – brought before them as a prisoner.

But this is their hour, and the power of darkness, permitted them by God that they might fill to the brim the cup of hate which they had so long been maturing against you; and might now at length openly give effect to their inveterate malice – to your honour and glory indeed, and for the salvation of the faithful, but for the eternal damnation of unbelievers.

I praise and glorify you, adorable Jesus, for so modestly standing before the High Priest and all the Elders of the people, who were impudently staring at your face which is deserving of all love. Grievous charges were, by the falsest of witnesses, laid against you; the high priest asked you many questions, adjuring you to answer truthfully; and at last, on a charge of blasphemy, you were declared to be guilty of death by them all, with loud voice.

I praise and magnify you, most noble Jesus, for each and every insult and falsehood levelled against you; for the lowly deference,

18

and the silence, which you did for so long a time maintain amidst the wicked charges of your accusers; at all which you made no sign of murmur or complaint, but did set before us all an example of perfect gentleness.

Ponder, then, O loving follower of Christ, and lay seriously to heart, how great was the splendour of the lowly patience of Jesus under suffering! See what shameful reproaches he has to bear whose praises are sung by the heavenly hosts! For his truthful answer to the High Priest's question he is condemned as a blasphemer. And yet, assuredly, all those who so condemn him proclaim themselves blasphemers, and guilty of an awful and stupendous crime. In the madness of their hearts, not believing him to be the Son of God, they wreak upon the Lord Jesus villainies of every kind; but he bears all in silence; and the more he allows himself to be trodden under foot of the ungodly, the greater is his victory and the greater is his triumph over them.

Cease, therefore, O faithful soul, from your passsionate murmurings at reproaches cast upon you, and from wishing to retaliate, and to be avenged, upon your adversaries. Bow down your back to sustain the burden of the earthly trials which come upon you; nor seek to prosper in a world, in which Christ was content to be despised. Blush, you proud one, at your honours, your high places, your magnificent retinue, and your fine clothing; seeing that for you Christ was content to be absolutely poor. A disgrace it surely is for you to covet the favours of men, and to hanker after earthly pleasures; for such desires are utterly at variance with a true following of Christ.

O most adorable Jesus, most meek, altogether lovely, grant to me, a miserable sinner, the grace of your favour, and teach me, by your shining example, not to be afraid of the threats and insults of the wicked, and not to be distressed at being unjustly accused; but rather to pray for the forgiveness of those who have wronged me, and to submit myself in all humility to you, and to my superiors; that so the gifts of your love may be more abundantly shed forth upon me, and I may have grace to praise you more earnestly for those already received.   **Amen.**

19

Jesus is mocked

Luke 22: 63-64

 bless you, and give thanks to you, O Lord Jesus Christ, crown and glory of the saints, for the grievous contempt, and the foul insults to which you were subjected, when, after you had been condemned to death, you were so shamefully abused and mocked with so many disgraceful words, by hard-hearted men, and were moreover frequently and roughly smitten on the head and face by them.

Oh, the thought that your altogether lovely countenance, upon which angels delight to look, should be basely dishonoured by the filthy spitting of men and be violently buffeted by the palms of their hands! Nor can we doubt that tears from your eyes mingled abundantly with the blood which was flowing from your nostrils. Your beauteous neck is sorely bruised by the blows rained upon it by the fists of those who smite you. Those eyes of yours, clear as crystal, which are ever over the righteous, are blindfolded in derision, like the eyes of fools. Your adorable head, exalted far above all creatures, is rudely struck by the polluted hands of sinners; and with mocking shouts they insult you, saying: 'Prophesy unto us, O Christ! Who is he that struck Thee?'

Who, O Lord, can hear of the indignities thus heaped upon you, without being moved to deep sorrow and anguish of heart? Of a truth your capacity for suffering far surpasses ours; but the hearts of those who love you cannot but be deeply wounded at the thought of all the shame and disgrace which you had to undergo. From your friends you were estranged; by your followers you were deserted; you were made a scoff and derision to them that hated you without a cause, who winked at you with their eyes. Ah, my Lord and my God, how can you suffer yourself to be thus mocked, and spitted on and buffeted by the ungodly as if you were the most foolish of men? Those raging Jews! All that night did they spend in mocking and in striking you; and yet, all the while, your unspeakable gentleness was unfailing, and although your impious tormentors could not discern it, the incomparable beauty of your soul was unchanged. To all your chosen ones, however, you have become still fairer and more precious, because, by the eye of faith, they recognize you as the most High God, and know that for love of them, all innocent as you were, you did suffer all these things.

I pray you, O most patient Jesus, that you would teach me, in my meditation on the surpassing insults heaped upon you, to realize my own vileness, and how by my sins I have richly deserved to be despised, and to be condemned amidst the scoffs and hisses of my fellow men. Pity my shortcomings, and strengthen me to bear harsh words spoken to me, even when I blush for shame at their violence. For because you were supremely humble, on behalf of me, a contemptible sinner, you endured, without complaining, and with supreme meekness, many despiteful words, besides bonds and stripes.

Oh how unlike you am I; how far from being truly humble am I, who for some trifling wrong or inconsiderate word, am angry with my fellow man; and, whereas I ought to be grateful for a reproof which was good for me, lose heart and feel impatient, and make no use of it!

Forgive, O Lord, I pray you, these my misdoings, and pardon my having so often offended you by my follies, my not having kept a pure conscience in my heart, and my not having shown towards you, and towards my fellow men, due humility and respect. Give me wholesome sorrow, and a fount of tears. Make me to welcome discipline, calling to mind the blows which you endured. Grant that even from the harshest charges brought against me, I may, by patience under them, win profit to my soul.   **Amen**.

21

Jesus before Pilate

Luke 23: 1-5

I bless you, and give thanks to you, O Lord Jesus Christ, most just Judge both of the living and of the dead, for the disorderly and noisy arraignment of you before Pilate, the Governor. For indeed, when morning was come the Chief Priests, having come together, and taken wicked counsel how they might put you to death, and having caused their attendants to bind you with cords, brought you before a man uncircumcised, a heathen Governor; and making against you, innocent as you were, the most grievous charges, dared to proclaim you, whom the holy prophets of old had hymned as Saviour of the world, a malefactor, and a perverter of their nation.

How dreadful was the wickedness of those Jews in seeking, upon the testimony of witnesses who were perjured, the condemnation of one who was innocent; in compassing the death of the author of life; in urging the crucifixion of Christ their King, and the putting to the most shameful of deaths of the Holy and Righteous One. May all your enemies, O Lord, be confounded, and put to shame; for they deserve far worse punishments than those which they meted out to you.

I praise and glorify you, adorable Jesus, for your perfect demeanour, and for the deference shown by you, when you were standing before the tribunal of Pilate, your judge; for you stood bound with cords, like a most meek lamb, in the presence of your accusers; with your head bent down; with your eyes fixed upon the ground; with your face calm; speaking but few words, and those in a soft voice; content to bear reproach, and even blows.

Behold, then, and lay to heart, O devout disciple of Christ, how your Lord and Saviour, who is the King and Judge of all men, submitting himself humbly, and of his own free-will, to the secular power, allows himself to be taken before the judgement-seat – in all which he has set before you an example. Submit yourself humbly to the judgement of your superiors; nor, if you would escape the pains of hell, venture to resist the power which is ordained of God: but, for the love of Jesus bear patiently an unjust condemnation, even if the punishment imposed be severe.

Let not the thought of the patience of your God – a patience shown when so many false charges were brought against him – pass from you, without leaving its mark upon your heart. Fall, then, at the sacred feet of Jesus bound with cords, and plead for pardon and grace; entreat his forgiveness for all your negligences, and that he will correct, in this your mercy's day, your offences, rather than, by reserving their punishment, cast you out for ever with the reprobates.

Have mercy upon me, O good Jesus; have mercy upon me, for my soul trusts in you. Breathe into me a right spirit, such as may kindle in me a fervent longing for progress in the inner life; so that I may strive with all my heart to humble myself, to give way and to submit to my superiors, and to bear all the burdens laid upon me. Grant that I may not stand in awe of men's judgements, and may not angrily defend myself against charges brought against me; rather, let me desire to be exercised, accused and disciplined that my pride may be trodden under foot and my own will be brought into subjection. In my self-abasement may I come to love you more and more and may I be carried further onward on the road to heaven.   **Amen**.

23

Herod exonerates Jesus

Luke 23: 6-12

 bless you, and give thanks to you, O Lord Jesus Christ, eternal wisdom of the Father; you who are Truth itself, and the infinite Power of God; for the foul insolence and bitter mockery, with which you were mocked and derided by Herod and his soldiers. For indeed Herod had himself for a long time been desirous to see you; and, moved by curiosity, was hoping to see some sign wrought by you. But when, to his questioning in many words, you answered nothing, and worked no sign – the time not being fit for so doing, because it was your hour for suffering, not for working miracles – soon, being moved to anger, he ceased to pay you respect, and treating you as a madman, insolently set you at nought; and having mocked you, by clothing you in a white garment, sent you back to Pilate.

I praise and magnify you, my glorious Jesus, for the fatigues you endured in being hurried about, as they led you, with shouts of derision, backward and forwards, from place to place, through the streets and lanes of Jerusalem, from judge to judge; before each of whom they defamed and grievously maligned you; and of whom at length, after you had been a long time examined and questioned, they demanded your punishment by crucifixion.

O how brightly shone forth in you at this time the patience, which was unmoved when goaded by such mockings. Surely the

24

thought of this public contempt cannot but touch deeply the hardest heart; cannot but assuage the wrath of the angriest; cannot but bring tears to the eyes of those who love you! You, the most High God, are brought as low as the lowest of mankind; you, the Almightly One, are rejected as one of no account; you, the All-Wise, are derided as a fool; you, the All-Holy, are adjudged to be the wickedest of men!

Woe to me, a miserable sinner, lying under a heavy burden of sin; for so far as my own merits are concerned I have deserved endless torments; and I would have had to endure them if you, my loving, holy, and just God had not condescended to be mocked and despised in order to save me from them and from everlasting death.

I beseech you, therefore, all-powerful Jesus, whom no malignant, no contemptuous words could provoke, that you would root out from me all vanity and daintiness, and that you would give me grace to be content with modest clothing; for it is a shameful thing that one, who is but dust and ashes, should wish to be clothed in handsome or soft garments, when you, the King of heaven, were content to be set at nought in a white garment.

Keep ever before my eyes the shame and the derision which you had to endure; teach me to follow you in willingness to be set at nought, and to be glad to be despised; teach me not to put my trust in the sons of men, nor in the princes of this world, not in what friends can do for me; teach me to despise all earthly good, and those who run after it; to follow, with a steadfastness from which nothing can turn me, you, O Lord Jesus, the author of my salvation; and ever to keep in remembrance the reproach which you endured for my sake, who am unworthy of the least of all your mercies. **Amen**.

LENT 14

'Crucify him'

Matt. 27: 15-26; John 18: 28-40; 19: 1-16

bless you, and give thanks to you, O Lord Jesus Christ, perpetual Joy of saints, for the great and insolent uproar with which the Jews raged against you, crying out in their fury: 'Away with Him! Away with Him! Crucify Him!' Alas, how great was the savagery of those miserable Jews; how inhuman was the cruelty of the priests and of the Pharisees, who felt no fear at putting you to death, who felt no compunction at shedding innocent blood! The heathen judge is moved to some sort of pity; but the hearts of the Jews are hardened to yet more cruel malice. Pilate would discharge you; he seeks to release you; he declares that he finds no cause of death in you; but the Jews, forgetting all the good works you had wrought among them, will not listen to him, crying out again: 'If thou release this man, thou art not Caesar's friend: for whosoever maketh himself a king, speaketh against Caesar.'

Alas, with what utter falseness they allege these things against you, who never, either by word or deed, sought earthly honours. After the miraculous feeding of the five thousand, the people sought to make you a king, but you went out alone to a mountain to pray, and to hide yourself from them!

Nor are these lies enough for them; they go on to add still worse, seeking at any cost to force the judge to put to death him who is very God. 'We have a law,' they say, 'and according to the law He ought to die, because He made Himself the Son of God.'

When the Governor hears these words, he fears the more, and asks: 'Whence art Thou?' And then he asks, 'What is truth?' But there is no answer; for the Jews are instant in demanding sentence of death. At length, anxious for the favour of princes, and led astray from the path of justice by the impious wickedness of the Jews, the Governor yields to their iniquitous demand.

What a sad and wicked thing it was that the words of execration, 'Crucify Him! Crucify Him!' spoken of the blessed Jesus, should have resounded through the streets of Jerusalem. Who of those who love him would not have mourned and wept, had he heard those accursed crucifixion cries repeated against his most loving Lord Jesus. What, then, must his most tenderly-loving Mother have felt, when those dreadful shouts, those death-dealing words, fell upon her ears; when that cruel doom, that tumultuous demand from the lips of all the people for the death of her Son upon the cross filled the air!

Weep with her, O faithful servant of Jesus, no matter of how little account you may be, weep with her, and draw forth from the recesses of your heart moans of sorrow and compassion. Try to think with what anguish the heart of Mary must have been torn, when she heard her blessed Son claimed for the shameful death of the cross.

He in whose ears ever resounds the angelic song, 'Holy! Holy!' ringing through the courts of heaven, has now to hear the accursed tongues of Jews acclaiming him with these words: 'Away with Him! Away with Him!' Only a short while ago on the Feast of Palms, the children had hailed him with songs of praise. Now these children's parents are madly demanding his crucifixion and shouting: 'Not this man but Barabbas.' What an awful change!

O you to whom the Passion of our Lord is dear, lay seriously to heart the thought of this hour, shut close the ears of your heart against profitless chatter about things of this world, and throw them open wide to hear this miserable outcry for the crucifixion of Jesus. Be sure, O faithful soul, that it will profit you more to meditate on it, than to know all about the wonders of the stars. If Jesus be indeed dear to you, you will not quit this theme without a bitter sigh. **Amen**.

Jesus is condemned

Matt. 27:26; Luke 23: 24-25

 bless you, and give thanks to you, O Lord Jesus Christ, author of life, and model of justice, for your unjust condemnation to death, although guilty of no offence at all; whilst a man guilty of murder and sedition, who had deserved sentence of death, was released. How perverse was such a judgement! How unjust was such an exchange! But when a mighty tumult was made by the people, and the judge saw that in no other way could he satisfy the ferocity of the Jews, he took his place upon the judgement seat, and pronounced against you the wicked sentence, that Barabbas the robber, who for a capital crime was worthy of death, should go scot-free; and that you, who were altogether guiltless, should be condemned to suffer that most shameful of deaths, the death of the Cross.

Of what sort, alas, is the judgement of this world, and how shockingly is justice trodden under foot when the wicked begin to have dominion! Behold how 'the just perisheth, and no man layeth it to heart!' Alas, alas, he who is Truth is delivered over to men who are false, the Holy One is scourged by sinners: he who is guiltless is condemned instead of him who is guilty: a robber is chosen instead of Christ: and Barabbas, who had been cast into prison, is set free instead of Jesus of Nazareth! The lamb takes the place of the wolf; the Holy One that of the malefactor; the best of men that of the worst; the man whose life was forfeit escapes, instead of him who is very God. Darkness is more highly esteemed than light, vice than virtue, death than life, clay than gold, a shell than a pearl, one who is infamous than one who is most noble.

Which of us on hearing these things can withhold a sigh? Which of us can help being angry with those Jews? Which of us can help blaming the judge? The judge may wash his hands, he may excuse himself before men; we may grant that he acted in fear of Caesar, and that he was overborne by the uproar of the Jews; yet is he not wholly free from guilt; for he knew that they had delivered him up out of envy. Better, surely, would it have been to have sacrificed high place, and the honours of this world, than to have condemned one who was innocent, and whom the Governor knew to be such. More profitable had it been to have lost the whole world, than to have sinned against God, and to have put Christ to death!

How terrible, at the last day, will be the judgement of the ungodly and unbelieving, when God the Judge, who is now condemned unjustly, shall have come in his glorious Majesty! Then shall they be joyous and free from care, who now patiently bear the hardships of this world, and submit to being wronged and despised.

O my sweet and loving Lord, who was unjustly condemned by Pilate the Governor, and sentenced to the shameful death of the Cross, grant that I may not take unduly to heart being put upon by one who is above me, but may always leave my cause in your hands: for the servant is not greater than his Lord; and if you, who are the Judge of all men, and were absolutely guiltless, made no resistance to the violence of your adversaries, but submitted to be unjustly condemned, how much more ought I to be ready to bear; and how cheerfully ought I to submit to the judgement of my brethren, whom I have, in so many ways, and so often, offended? Help me, O gracious Lord Jesus, willingly to bear the yoke of subjection, and the rod of correction, and in every trouble that comes upon me, to call to mind your anguish. **Amen**.

Jesus is scourged

Matt. 27: 27-31

I bless you, and give thanks to you, O Lord Jesus Christ, most kind protector of all who hope in you, for the shame you endured in being stripped naked, in the sight of those who mocked you. By the cruel order of the wicked Governor, you were ordered to be stripped by the Roman soldiers of your clothing, and to be hung upon the Cross quite naked, to be bound with hard cords, to be beaten with sharp-cutting rods, and to be scourged as if you had been a wicked seducer of the people, and the vilest of malefactors – all which was done to conciliate the wrath of the priests, who sought to glut themselves with your blood, and to bring you down with sorrow to the grave.

I laud and magnify, and humbly praise you, especially for the fast binding to the stony pillar, which you endured, so that you might loose us from the bonds of our sins, and might restore to us that freedom which knows no end.

I praise and glorify you with thanksgivings which shall never cease, for your most cruel scourging; and for each of the hard stripes, and most sharply cutting wounds, inflicted on your most sacred and tender body by those fierce soldiers who mercilessly struck your virgin flesh, and rent it deeply, addding blow to blow, bruise upon bruise so that there might remain no sound part in you, and that at each stroke numberless streams of your precious blood might gush forth like those of a crimson river – all which you endured that you might purge us from the deep-rooted pollutions of our sins, and might cleanse our souls from every guilty stain by your own most precious blood.

Alas, alas, O Lord my God, how great was the fury of those angry Jews. What hearts of stone were those of the men who struck you, who shrank not from scourging you, the fairest of men, all sinless as you were; but reared themselves like giants over you, and did their very worst against you! . . .

O altogether sweet Jesus, who for me, the chief of sinners, was most cruelly scourged, grant that I may gaze with a heart full of sorrow upon each wound made upon your sacred body by the scourge, and that I may kiss it with heartfelt fervent love; and so may feel the savour of life, and the medicine of eternal salvation, flowing forth from thence upon me. Set me aflame with the fire of that boundless love, with which you proved that you loved me, when you vouchsafed most patiently to endure so many blows of the cruel scourge for me, your servant lying under condemnation.

When tribulation of any kind comes upon me, grant, I pray you, to my weakness the help of your grace; so that I may not be cast down under its burden, nor be too much distressed by it; but, remembering your undeserved scourging, may be found meek and submissive under what I have to bear, no matter how heavy it may be. Make me a partner in your sufferings and stir me up to amendment of life by the chastening of sons, that so, by bearing punishment with due meekness and humility, I may in this present life become more pleasing to you, and in the life to come may rejoice with you more gloriously, in that place, where all your saints, no longer in fear of sin, rejoice for ever in the victory which your sufferings have won for them. **Amen.**

Jesus is crowned with thorns

Mark 15: 16-20

bless you, and give thanks to you, O Lord Jesus Christ, illustrious King of saints, and shining crown of everlasting glory, for the many unheard-of outrages and affronts, to which you were once more subjected by your impious tormentors, when you were brought by the cruel soldiers into the Praetorium. There, the whole band being gathered together unto you, you were shamefully stripped of your own garments, and instead of them, were mockingly clothed in a scarlet cloak; so that you might clothe us, who are devoid of all goodness, with the cloak of your own holiness, and might adorn us with the sweetness of your own nature.

I praise and glorify you, with the special devotion of a heart full of compassion, for the very great pain you had to bear for us poor earthly creatures, when the crown of thorns was forced upon your sacred head. For at that time your ever-blessed head was oppressed by such a multitude of thorns, and was so grievously pierced, even down to the brain itself, that large streams of blood ran down everywhere over your neck and ears, over your eyes and cheeks, and made your sweet face, which was as yet scarce dry from the spitting of the Jews, bloody and disfigured.

O sight of all sights the saddest; to see the Son of God, in whom no spot of sin could be found, so ignominiously and so cruelly crowned!

How surpassingly cruel was the rage of the soldiers, who shrank not from piercing with so many thorn-points that head, so noble and so worshipful; and who even dared to insult the king of angels by saluting him in mockery, by smiting him, and by making him a laughing-stock to the multitude!

I laud and magnify you, for the mocking salutation, and pretended respect, shown to you; when your tormentors, bowing the knee before you, struck you on the head; when they contemptuously adored you, and ironically styling you king, acclaimed you in the words: 'Hail, King of the Jews!'

I praise and bless you, my adorable Jesus, for the despiteful mockery which you endured, when, to add to your distress, a frail reed was put into your right hand instead of a royal sceptre; as if to proclaim you an audacious pretender to kingly rank.

I laud and magnify you for the most cruel smitings of your already wounded head, which you endured when those pitiless men and most brutal tormentors, lifting high the reed, struck you many blows with it on the top of your sacred head; and, yet again covering you with loathsome spittle from their filthy mouths, thrust out their tongues at you.

O most gentle Jesus, King deserving of all love, crown of confessors, stay of the Church militant, joy of the Church triumphant, model for all who would follow you, how outrageously you were treated, how cruelly you were tormented; outwardly what affronts are heaped on you; inwardly with what unspeakable distress are you filled – and all for my sake; that you might save me from being confounded for ever, in the torments of hell; that you might pluck out from my heart the thorns, which my sins have left in it; and that you might crown me, in the heavenly mansions, with a crown of glory and of honour that fades not away!   **Amen**.

LENT 18

Jesus bears his Cross

John 19: 17-18

 bless you, and give thanks to you, O Lord Jesus Christ, true Vine, Way of Life, and our salvation, for bearing before all men your heavy and shameful Cross. For the salvation of the whole human race, you vouchsafed humbly to take it up, and most patiently to bear it; so that, upon your own shoulders, you might bring back, to your home in heaven, the lost sheep you so long sought after, and found with so much toil and trouble.

I laud and magnify you, illustrious standard-bearer of the Christian army, for your sorrowful and distressing journey, when, with the heavy wood of the cross roughly laid upon you, you were ignominiously led forth outside the walls of that renowned city, in which you had so often manifested forth your glory by miracles worked, and holy doctrine taught therein. Now, however, amid the furious outcries of the whole people arrayed against you, you are treated as a comrade of thieves, and a chief of robbers, and are going forth to be hanged, as one utterly vile and worthless, upon the highest cross of all, between two of the worst of malefactors.

I praise and glorify you, most gracious Jesus, for that cruel and most wearisome progress, for that journey amid such horrible surroundings, which you undertook for us. I praise and glorify you for each step you took; for the exceeding weariness and weakness of your body, caused by your previous sufferings; for the ascents and descents of the winding road, made more grievous to you by the burden of your Cross; for the haste with which you were at one time urged forward from behind, and at another time dragged roughly on from in front, by the hard-hearted men of the guard in charge of you; hither and thither buffeted about by them. For you could only move with your body bent almost double from the weight of that burden, so far beyond your strength, which you were compelled to bear to the hill of Calvary. Never before had you trodden so cruel a road; never before had you borne so grievous a yoke.

I laud and magnify you for the despiteful usage you had to endure from those brutish men who led you forth to execution, at one time abusing you, at another ill-treating you. Amidst all which horrors, heaped upon you from every side, you went as a meek lamb carried forth for sacrifice, having before you our salvation as your aim; pitying the blindness of the Jews; and sorrowing over the malice of those who were leading you to the place of execution.

O my dearly loved Jesus, Prince of the kings of the earth, leader of the angelic host, illustrious standard-bearer of all Christians, who, for the salvation of your servants, and that you might set them a perfect example, bore your Cross upon your own shoulders amidst the jeers and scoffs of the Jews who surrounded you, grant me grace, slow of heart though I be, to follow you along your weary road; be with me to the end; and then lead, I pray you, my soul, now absent from its true home, from this body of sin to the mount of Calvary, the hill of myrrh and frankincense, where you were, for my sake, crucified and slain, that there I may rest under the shadow of your Cross, safe beneath its holy sign.

Grant that I may now make a fresh start, and may follow you, not with the infirmity of purpose of those who are neither hot nor cold, but with renewed fervour of heart; keeping my eyes steadily fixed upon you, the Cross-bearer, and not letting them stray hither and thither like those who are inconstant in their ways. Be my guide along the narrow road, and my companion as I follow it: be at hand to help me when things are going well with me, to comfort me when they are going wrong, to sustain me in all the trials which I may have to undergo for the sake of your holy name. **Amen**.

LENT 19

Jesus is crucified

Matt. 27: 33-36

I bless you, and give thanks to you, O Lord Jesus Christ, most gracious fashioner of man, and restorer of his fallen nature, for the shame of nakedness endured by you at the foot of the Cross, when before the eyes of the mob who, like beasts of prey howling for their food, were roaring at you, you were stripped of your clothes, and put to open shame. After all your clothes had been roughly taken from you, and had been given away as a prize, there you stood blushing, trembling, girt only about the loins with a thin linen cloth, and crowned, instead of a diadem, with a garland of thorns, set at nought of men and utterly despised and rejected.

There did you stand, absolutely stripped of this world's goods, as an outcast of the people and a poverty-stricken alien, nay rather as the very poorest of the poor, bereft of everything and of every human consolation. For as, in the garden of Eden, before Paradise was lost, the first Adam went naked; so now you too, in like manner, ascend the Cross naked, to regain for us that lost Paradise, from which Adam was cast out, and driven forth. For it was in order that the innocence which had been lost might be restored to fallen man; and in order that he might be clad in a robe of righteousness, and might be made an heir of everlasting life, that you submitted to be deprived of your clothing, to be overwhelmed with anguish and distress, and in the end to pay the penalty of a most cruel death.

I praise and magnify you, who desire all men to be saved, for the merciless way in which you were stretched out upon the hard

36

wood of the Cross, so roughly spread for you as your reclining-board; for the sharp piercing of your hands and feet, and for the driving into them of huge nails, the noise caused by which could be heard far off, and must have moved to tears even the most hard-hearted of the beholders. You were, also, so firmly nailed to the Cross that your veins suddenly burst, and streams of your precious blood poured forth from all parts of your body.

So ruthlessly, indeed, was your body stretched out lengthwise and breadthwise, as if it had been the skin of a drum, that all your joints wre loosened, and your bones could be distinctly counted. You allowed your hands and your feet to be pierced by the ungodly, in order that by having your sacred hands fastened to the Cross, you might discharge the debt incurred by Adam in stretching forth wicked hands to touch the forbidden tree; and, by shedding your innocent blood, might wipe out the long-standing obligation of a sacrifice for sin.

I praise and glorify you for being lifted up on high upon the Cross, and for remaining hung so long upon the arms of that tree of shame – the tree which was at that time held by all Jews to be accursed, but is now held in supreme honour by all Christians, and blessed above every tree that grows. For our salvation, you hung, for three full hours or more, working out those great and wonderful mysteries of the Cross, from which were to flow such inestimable benefits for all the world.

You were lifted up from the earth that you might draw up after you the loving hearts of those who believe in you, and prevent their leading a mere butterfly life in pursuit of earthly joys; that, by commiserating your sufferings, the tender hearts of your faithful ones might become yet more tender, and, at the sight of you upon your Cross, their love might burn still brighter; that in your own Person, you might triumph fully and openly over the evil powers of the air; that by thus humbling yourself, you might make for transgressors intercession which could not fail of being heard, and might assure to the truly penitent full and free forgiveness of their sins; and that, by your death, you might reconcile the things which are in heaven and the things which are in earth, and might make all things new. **Amen**.

Jesus on the Cross

Luke 23:33

ook, O heavenly Father, upon the face of your Christ, as he hangs upon the Cross for me; and for the sake of the all-sufficient merits of your only-begotten Son, pierced with nails, and besprinkled with blood, be merciful to me a sinner, tied and bound with the chains of so many sins. For he was wounded to blot out my iniquities; he will make satisfaction to you for all my sins; he will answer to you in my stead. I offer him to you as my Surety; I choose him as my Advocate; I put him forward as my Mediator; to him I leave the defence of my cause.

He will make good all in which I have fallen short; he, the blessed fruit of the Virgin's womb, will fully atone for all my transgressions of your commands. O most merciful Father, you will surely take pleasure in accepting his pleading on my behalf; and thus, on account of his exceeding love, and great desire for my eternal salvation, I may always feel that hope and consolation, which in this life are profitable for me, and without which, in the life to come, I must needs be undone.

O good and tender Jesus, all-holy Son of God, who, in fulfilment of your Father's will, vouchsafed to take upon you, without any spot of sin, the substance of our flesh, and to offer the same upon the altar of the Cross for the salvation of the world, have mercy upon me, your servant, who pray to you for pardon and for grace. Of your goodness, and for the infinite merit of your Passion, forgive, I beseech you, all my sins, whether new or old, whether committed against you knowingly, or unknowingly. Your merits far outweigh the sins of all mankind; and the fullness of your atonement far exceeds my every sin, no matter how often committed.

To you, therefore, do I flee for refuge, invoking the protection of your Cross, to which I trust for mercy greater than all my need; to you, from the bottom of my heart, do I cry, beseeching you to help me, and to save me. I venerate the sign of the Cross, I honour the banner of the Cross; I kiss the foot of the Cross, and I invoke the aid of the Cross. Listen to me in my distress; receive me, who flee to you for help; heal me, who come to you in contrition of heart; justify me a sinner. Till I am taken back into your favour, I will not leave you, nor let you go.

Root out of my heart, I pray you, O my crucified Lord Jesus, all love for the things of this world. Take me by the arms, and raise me to the height of your Cross; let me follow you whithersoever you go. With you at hand, and keeping close to you, and so lifted up above all earthly things, gladly will I share your poverty and nakedness, passing my life in this world as an exile and unknown.

Implant in my flesh reverence for you, lest I give way to sloth or laziness; transfix my feet, so that I may steadfastly persevere, and may bravely endure toil and sorrow. May your nails be driven through the centre of my heart, and rack me with a wholesome wound, so that I may shed abundant tears of true contrition, and be, as it were, beside myself with the intensity of my love. Inspire me with sorrow, increase my devotion, till nothing is dearer to me, and nothing closer to my heart than Jesus Christ, and him crucified. **Amen**.

Jesus's garments are divided

Mark 15: 24; John 19: 23-24

 bless you, and give thanks to you, O Lord Jesus Christ, maker of all things, and giver of all good things, for the rude plundering and the mocking partition of your garments; when, as soon as you had been cruelly nailed to your Cross, you were savagely despoiled of all your clothing, and driven forth disinherited even to the last cent; so that not even a stitch of clothing was left wherewith to cover your nakedness, nor even a piece of linen for a shroud, in which after your death you might be wrapped, and be decently laid in your grave.

If you are not to go to your grave naked, a winding-sheet will have to be obtained for you from strangers, and will have to be given as an act of kindness to one utterly poor and destitute. How hungry was the covetousness of those soldiers – soldiers indeed, nay rather low vagabonds! How shameless was the rapacity of those base men of the guard set over him, who in their unholy greed were not shamed of despoiling Jesus of his scraps of worldly goods; but sated, as best they might, their thirst for gain by making the meagre garments of the Crucified their prey! Having taken his garments, they made of them four parts, to every soldier a part, leaving entire the coat only, because it had no seam; and for it they cast lots, because they could not share it otherwise without wasting it.

Alas for the wickedness of those robbers! Alas for the spite of those extortioners, who had not even so much pity for Jesus hanging on the Cross, poor and naked, as to give him back some little thing, or to leave even a shred of one of his garments for his sorrowing mother to keep as a remembrance of him whom she had lost! Not one of these things did they, because urged on by the devil, they were working out their sacrilege, without thought of a judgement to come.

To think of the supreme Creator of heaven, true God, and true Man, reduced to such straits as this! At his birth he had scarcely a few poor rags to cover him, and now at his death, he has no clothes at all! Then a narrow manger held his infant limbs; now deprived of all his worldly goods, he has, in all the world which he created, no place to lay his head except his Cross; for as he came into the world poor and needy, so now he willed to leave it naked and an outcast. At his birth he was tightly wrapped in swaddling-clothes; at his death he is pierced by lance and nails.

The thought of so great misery calls surely for compassion; the showing forth of so great patience calls surely for imitation. Be, then, more patient than ever before, when things that seem needful to you are taken from you, or when things upon which you have set your heart are denied you. Learn to do with little, and to be content with what is mean and poor; so shall you be kept from grumbling, and shall have peace in yourself and favour with Almightly God.

O Jesus, King of kings, at once the richest and the poorest of men, O Lord most poor, as stripped of your clothes, and deserted by your friends; but at the same time most rich in the fullness of your spiritual gifts; grant, I beseech you, to me, your poor servant, out of the abundance of your excellences, to have one at least in its fullness, that, namely, of not being found naked and ashamed before you, like the man who was found at the marriage supper not having on a wedding garment, and was later, for this defect, cast out from the company of the saints. May my heart be torn to pieces by a wholesome sorrow for sin, in remembrance of the tearing of your garment into four parts, so that by one at least out of four motives I may be moved to repentance; by fear of hell, by hope of future glory, by sorrow for past sin, or by thankful love for grace given me. **Amen**.

Jesus sheds his precious blood

John 19:34

 Lord Jesus Christ, author of our salvation, most gracious giver of pardon, most patient in your long-suffering of man's wickedness, I bless you, and give thanks to you for all the pain, and for each several blow and bloody wound, so cruelly inflicted on your most precious and most tender body; so that from the sole of the foot even to the top of the head there was no soundness in you but either a grievous weal, or an aching wound, or a stream of warm red blood trickling down your whole body.

I praise and glorify you with the worthiest adoration of which I am capable, and with all the powers of my soul laid at your feet, for the generous outpouring of your precious blood from your five sacred wounds, and from all other wounds, great and small, bleeding and sending forth a life-giving stream, more precious than any balm, to be an effectual remedy for all our sins. Ah! most gentle Jesus, how cruelly were you tortured and wounded by savage men, so that all your bodily strength being exhausted, and your veins wide-opened, scarcely a drop of blood remained in you; but whatever of that sacred stream, whether living or dying, you had in you, was all lovingly poured forth for our souls' use, and as the price of our salvation.

O five precious wounds, pre-eminent tokens of surpassing love, full of divine sweetness, from you the sinner takes good heart, keeping thereby his guilty conscience from driving him to despair! In you is found the medicine of life, fullness of grace, plentiful forgiveness, boundless mercy, the gate which leads to the glory which is in store for us. Whatever pollution I incur, whatever sins of the flesh I commit, in your five fountains I may wash all away, and may be purified, and made faultless.

Many faithful souls, burning with love for Jesus, have rejoiced to shed their blood for him: and yet more, taking part in his sufferings by using the rough ways of penance, have, for the chalice of his blood, humbly offered the waters of a bitter contrition.

Learn from their example to crucify your flesh with its affections and lusts, manfully to resist temptation, and to bear until death the yoke of willing obedience; to offer to Christ your Redeemer, upon the altar of your heart, in place of a martyrdom of blood, the sacrifice of a troubled spirit. Seek by diligent meditation to keep ever before you the benefits purchased for you by the Cross, and to find in the deep wounds of Jesus, as in the clefts of a rock, a hiding-place from the face of the enemy and the avenger.

Come to my help, O most gentle Jesus, in my every need, in every crisis of the strife. Stretch forth over me your hands, and with your right arm ever protect me; put devotion in my heart, truth in my mouth, energy in my work. Purge me from all the corruption of my sins, heal my wounds with your precious blood. Let no hidden thing of darkness, nothing impure, nothing that defiles, remain in me; but may your sacred blood, so abundantly shed, thoroughly cleanse me from all that is hurtful, and sanctify me wholly; so that, when at the last day, you shall come in judgement, my spirit, and my soul, for which you endured so many and such grievous pains, and expended such boundless treasure, may be presented before you pure and undefiled. **Amen**.

Jesus prays for his enemies

Luke 23: 33-34

bless you, and give thanks to you, O Lord Jesus Christ, fountain of love and sweetness, for your most perfect charity, and most devoted prayer on behalf of your enemies, and of those who were crucifying you. With your hands stretched out upon the cross you pleaded for them, imploring pardon for them, and making loving excuses for them, in the words: 'Father, forgive them, for they know not what they do' – words so full of sweetness and of love that they might well have softened the heart of the most hardened of sinners, and have led him to repent. O most sweet Jesus, how ready are you to forgive, how easily are you appeased, how plenteous you are in mercy!

How vast, O my Lord, must be the stores of your tender mercies towards those who love you, when you could show forth such loving kindness towards your savage enemies; when, raised aloft upon your Cross, you were not moved to anger against your crucifiers, and did not seek to be revenged upon your tormentors; did not pray that the earth might swallow up alive those wicked men, or that fire from heaven might consume them in a moment; but you did shed forth upon your cruel enemies, like healing dew from heaven, the words: 'Father, forgive them, for they know not what they do.' In this was manifested your most excellent charity and your unspeakable tenderness, which nothing could overcome, nothing could hold back from loving intercession. They were crying out: 'Crucify Him, crucify Him!' and you were saying: 'Father, forgive them.' They pierced you with hard nails, and you made excuses for their foul iniquities, in the words: 'For they know not what they do.' O Christ, how wondrous is your love!

They did you all the harm they could; and you repaid them by doing for them your best. The best and most loving thing you could do for men so wicked, was to pray that they might be turned from their evil ways, and might confess that you, the Son of God, had truly come in the flesh. And thus were fulfilled those memorable words of Isaiah, which of old he had spoken concerning you: 'And He hath borne the sins of many, and hath prayed for the transgressors,' that they may not perish.

O most gracious Lord Jesus, who of your infinite love vouchsafed to pray for your enemies, vouchsafe, I beseech you, in the same spirit of charity, to pray the Father for me, that he will grant me full pardon for all my sins, and will of his great mercy deliver me from the punishments which they have deserved. Grant that I may have a perfect and unwavering trust in your love and mercy, and that I may not give way to despair on account of the greatness of my sins; but may remember, in the full assurance of faith, that you came into the world to save sinners, and willed to suffer, to be crucified, and to die, for the ungodly.

May, then, that prayer for your enemies, which, in fulfilment of this your blessed purpose, you prayed upon your Cross, bear fruit to the salvation of my soul; and grant to me, I pray, a sure hope of obtaining pardon through it; so that I may be found meet to obtain, through your most holy intercession, that which by my own merits I could never hope to win. Grant me boldly and fearlessly to seek refuge under the shadow of your wings, and to be kept by the invincible sign of your holy Cross from all fear of the old enemy. As I haste to lay hold upon your Cross, spread over me, I beseech you, the shelter of your arms; so that, whenever my last hour shall come, my helpless and sorrowing soul may neither be afraid nor despair; and take me, I pray you, to yourself, a miserable sinner, trusting not at all to my own works, but solely to your great mercy. **Amen**.

Jesus is reviled

Mark 15: 22-32; Luke 23: 33-39

 bless you, and give thanks to you, O Lord Jesus Christ, who are the glory and the crown of rejoicing of the citizens of heaven, for all the reproaches and blasphemies hurled at you by the faithless Jews, as you hung on your Cross. From the least of them to the greatest they took part against you, and came running together to devour your innocency. With their lips they cursed you; with their faces they mocked you; they clapped with their hands; they danced with their feet, they rejoiced in their hearts; because they had you before them, hanging on the Cross – you whom they would not willingly let die without being harassed and insulted.

O most cruel and most savage persecutors of the Son of God, why were you not content with perpetrating the horrible crime of the crucifixion? Why must you add to your sins that of blaspheming and deriding the Son of God? Alas! Alas! what are you doing? Why sharpen your venomous tongues upon One so loving and so spotless? Wherein has he sinned; or in what has Christ at any time done you harm? Has he not done all things well, who has made both the deaf to hear, and the dumb to speak? Has he not made your whole land famous by many excellent miracles, and by his doctrine full of sweetness and grace? Did he not pray even for his enemies? What evil recompense did he deserve for all these things? Why do you return evil for good, and hatred for love? It would have been more fitting, by way of expiating so great wickedness, that you should have shed tears, than that you should have laughed in the face of the Crucified. But alas, you know not, neither do you care.

In stubborn hearts there is found no place for compassion, nor for contrition, nor for thought of benefits received; nay, rather a devilish madness, breaking out in yet more bitter taunts and insults, ever urges such men on to more atrocious crimes. Being no longer able to wreak their vengeance by means of swords and clubs, they set to work to use the even sharper weapons of their tongues.

And now, in the same way, the soldiers, to whom was committed the execution of the cruel sentence, proud of the work assigned them, knowing nothing of the Law of God, and made worse by the attentions and the encouragement of the rulers of the people, go nearer to the Cross, and in mockery offer vinegar to the Crucified, saying: 'If Thou be the King of the Jews, save Thyself!' You stupid soldiers, base in your manners and in your deeds, who has taught you so to fight that you should war against God? It is not the work of gallant men to persecute One who is holy, One who is poor; to leave naked One who has been robbed, to tear his garments in pieces, to mock the Crucified, to offer vinegar (which no man likes to drink) to God who is about to die. Nevertheless you cannot harm Christ: for wisdom overcomes malice, and the patience of Jesus no insults can exhaust.

The thief, too, who hung on the left hand, and remained impenitent in his sin, joined in these reproaches, saying: 'If Thou be Christ, save Thyself, and us.' That unhappy man, alas, treats you with contempt, and plunges into an abyss of horrors. Instead of praying, as he should, for forgiveness of his evil deeds, he insulted you, O Christ, the bestower of pardon. And so, the wretched man met his death in despair and perished miserably.

I praise and glorify you for your unflinching steadfastness in clinging to the Cross to which you had submitted yourself, and from which no revilings, no specious suggestions, could move you to descend—not even for one short moment would you leave that Cross upon which, of your own free will, you had been raised on high. It was your will there to abide to the end, where of your exceeding love you had placed yourself; there to remain and to die, and there to consummate, in a way fitted to accomplish your purpose, the work which for our sakes you had begun.

Grant that I may ever be patient in adversity, and may not fear the taunts of men, nor seek to win their praise; that I may turn away my eyes from the things of this life, and may look for all my comfort to you, my only Saviour. **Amen.**

47

Jesus addresses the thief

Luke 23: 39-43

I bless you, and give thanks to you, O Lord Jesus Christ, chief and only comfort of sinners, for the boundless love and exceeding mercy, which you vouchsafed to show to him who hung at your right hand upon his cross. He had been a most wicked thief, but was now at length converted, and a true penitent. As soon as he acknowledged his sinfulness, and was truly sorry for his evil deeds, he obtained, by your sure promise, remission of all his sins, and entrance into Paradise; for when a man's contrition is true, and his conversion complete, his repentance, however late it may be, will not fail of its reward.

How blessed and life-giving are the conversion and contrition of sinners, by which, without delay, a man may gain a place in the kingdom of heaven! That penitent, who had been a thief, but was now a blessed confessor, although he had long and grievously sinned, yet at last, and in the hour of his greatest need, came to himself; and grieving with heartfelt sorrow for all that he had done, humbly sought forgiveness, and obtained full pardon. For when he owned that he was justly condemned to death, he admitted that he had been guilty. He had a zeal for righteousness, when he reproved his comrade at his side for the wickedness of his blasphemy. He shows that his heart is in its right place, when he laments that Christ, who is altogether free from guilt, has been unjustly condemned. He had great faith; for he did not despair of obtaining mercy from Christ; but asked to be remembered by him in the kingdom of God: and so, being full of the gifts of grace, he appealed, in the full assurance of faith, to you, O Lord Jesus, whom he owned as the loving Shepherd of souls, the true Priest, and the Confessor of all confessors the most faithful; and having in his mind's eye the whole course of his life, he said: 'Lord, remember me when Thou shalt come into Thy Kingdom.' And you, O most gracious Jesus, answered him in those most sweet and most comforting words: 'Amen, I say to thee, this day thou shalt be with Me in paradise.'

How comforting and wholesome a thing it is for me to consider thoughtfully the circumstances of this thief's death, and of your most sweet answer to his prayer; not in order that I may be more fearless in sinning, or may put off amendment longer than I should; but that I may learn, when suddenly overcome by temptation, that I need not despair. Although he had been such an evildoer, he was suddenly converted and made an heir, by your merciful grace, of everlasting life, and restored to Paradise.

I should indeed, O Lord, be sorely troubled on account of my many sins, did I not know of your mercies, had I not heard of cases of penitents most graciously taken back into your favour. It is you who by the mouth of your prophet said: 'I would not the death of a sinner, but rather that he should be converted and live': and again by your own mouth: 'God so loved the world as to give His only-begotten Son; that whosoever believeth in Him, may not perish, but may have life everlasting': and again: 'I am not come to call the just, but sinners.' It was you who forgave to Mary Magdalene all her sins without delay as she knelt weeping at your feet. It was you who took back into your favour Peter, who had thrice denied you, when he went out and wept bitterly. It was you who, in your mercy, healed those who were taken with divers diseases, and, in the abundance of your love, you loosed those who were bound with the chain of very grievous sins – witness the woman taken in adultery, whom you saved from the hands of her accusers, who were about to stone her.

O most gracious Jesus, my hope of mercy, and my refuge; you undertake for me, and deliver me from my cruel enemies; be merciful to me, and suffer not my soul to perish, to redeem which you were content to endure the shameful death of the Cross. Remember your sacred words spoken to the thief, by which to me also you have left a hope so firm that it can never be shaken. Say, then, to my soul, O Saviour of my life, when the hour of my departure shall draw near: 'This day thou shalt be with Me in Paradise.' **Amen.**

The title of Jesus

John 19: 19-22

I bless you, and give thanks to you, O Lord Jesus Christ, Prince of almighty power, and King of every creature, for the illustrious title of your holy and blessed name, openly displayed above your head. It was carefully written, by Pilate the Governor, in the three most renowned languages of the world, in letters of Hebrew and Greek and Latin, in this form, and in these words: JESUS OF NAZARETH, THE KING OF THE JEWS.

O title truly illustrious, not in the creation of man's ingenuity, but rather of divine ordinance, foreseen, and dictated by God, from all eternity. Pilate, indeed, could not, and ought not, to have written otherwise than as he was inspired to write; and so it is that the mystic sense of this title is found in the famous Scriptures of the prophets expressed in their own words. What, therefore, the sacred page had long before predicted, what clear tradition had handed down along the ages, in praise of your life-giving name, that the heathen Governor, inspired by God, wrote upon a small tablet, as an everlasting memorial of the Crucified, in these words: 'Jesus of Nazareth, King of the Jews.'

When, therefore, many of the Jews had read this title, the priests, in the fury of their ill-will, could not bear that the glory of your name, which they had been struggling with all their might to obscure, should be thus proclaimed to the world: and so they came to Pilate the Governor with their complaints as to the honour needlessly conferred by such a title, saying: 'Write not, the King of the Jews; but that He said: I am the King of the Jews.' For they feared that they would be confounded, and that their wicked cruelty in having crucified their King would be laid to their charge; and to prevent this being any longer spread abroad, they asked to have the title changed, so that

Jesus might not appear to have been crucified on account of their malice; but that he might rather seem to have been condemned as a pretender to a throne, and because he, who had never in this world exercised any royal authority, had dared to say that he was a king.

O brave Governor, your inscription was very good, and your answer to those priests was just. I praise you for having framed so holy and beautiful a title for the Cross of Jesus of Nazareth, and for having so boldly put the Jews to silence: but in this I praise you not, that you consented to the death of Christ – in so doing you grievously sinned.

O Jesus of Nazareth, bright flower of the virgin Mary; O illustrious Son of David, the Only-Begotten of the supreme Father, write, I pray you, with a strong and clear hand, upon the tablets of my heart, your sweet and glorious name, along with that sacred and brightly-shining title of your Passion, which declared the cause of your death; so that I may keep it ever before my eyes, and may often read it to the praise of your most holy name. May that title be the comfort of my heart in distress; may it be my special protection when temptations assail me; may the evil spirit depart from me; may the lust of concupiscence die out within me; may the whole world have a bitter taste to me, when I think, or read, of 'Jesus of Nazareth, the King of the Jews.'

For of a truth nothing is more sweet that Jesus, nothing more wholesome, nothing more helpful; nothing can be brighter, nothing more pure, nothing more holy than the Nazarene; nothing can be more worthy of honour than the King of the Jews, nothing more powerful, nothing more exalted. Therefore, let no enemy think to withstand me; let no plague think to touch me; let no calamity think to crush me, so long as I humbly invoke your aid, O my Jesus, or call to mind your Passion, or dwell with heart and lips upon your title 'Jesus of Nazareth, the King of the Jews.'

O Jesus, above all else deserving of my love, you are my King and my God, dear to me above everything, far above all the praise that I can give you. Dear to me were you in the manger, still dearer were you on the Cross; dearest of all are you when sitting upon the throne of your kingdom; for though, in the weakness of your flesh, you hung upon the Cross, yet now by the power of God, you live, and are sitting at the right hand of the Father, exalted above every creature for ever and ever. **Amen**.

Jesus entrusts Mary to John

John 19: 25-27

bless you, and give thanks to you, O Lord Jesus Christ, comforter of all that mourn, for the sorrowful glance which, in your mercy, you cast upon your dearly-loved mother as she stood beneath your Cross, worn out with the intensity of her grief. How intense that grief was, you alone best knew, from whom the most secret motions of her heart were not hid; for, upon earth, there was nothing more dear to you than your virgin mother; and she loved nothing so much as you, her God and her Son.

Although you were the fruit of her womb, she knew, without doubt, that you were her maker and the Lord of all things. When, therefore, she saw you, whom she loved above all else, hanging upon the Cross, her heart was in you, rather than in herself; and being lifted, as it were, outside herself, she will, in spirit, have hung with you upon the Cross, even when, in the body, she was standing weeping at its foot.

I praise and glorify you for the exceeding great compassion with which, as a Son, you grieved with your most sorrowful mother, to whom all your anguish was as if it had been her own; who wept over each wound of yours as if it had been inflicted upon herself; and whose heart was racked with fresh pain as often as, with a mother's eye, she saw blood flowing from your body, or heard your voice as you spoke to her from the Cross.

I laud and magnify you for those most gracious words, few in number though they were, which you finally spoke to your disconsolate mother. You commended her to your wellbeloved disciple John, as to a most faithful steward, and brought together in an indissoluble bond of love Mary and him who was vowed to chastity, saying to her: 'Woman, behold thy son,' and then to your disciple: 'Behold thy mother.'

O happy union, and pleasing commendation, shared and consecrated by virgin purity! For in these words you showed on the one hand your loving care for your mother's honour, by giving her the protection of your chaste disciple, and on the other hand, you filled your vacant place by assigning to her another son. By the chastity of his life he was suited to give her a home, and he might be depended on to provide her with the necessaries of life. You did what your feeling as a son prompted you to do so that Mary, your holy mother, might always have a faithful attendant; and when deprived of your most sweet presence, might never feel as if she were left alone in the world, and as a stranger among the Jews.

Most blessed John did as Jesus had bidden him from the Cross. From that hour the disciple took her to his home, watched over her, carefully ministered to her, most faithfully submitted himself to her, and loved her with his whole heart, as if she had been his own mother.

Be glad and rejoice, O blessed Saint John, in the trust committed to you: for what in all the world Christ held most dear, that he made over to your care. He gave you great wealth, when he bequeathed to you Mary, whom even the holy angels cannot worthily praise. To Saint Peter Christ gave charge of the keys of the kingdom of heaven, but he made you his own mother's chamberlain. Formerly Mary was betrothed to holy Joseph, but now she is entrusted to you as to her second guardian.

Take, then, the holy mother of Christ into your care; for by her words you shall be instructed, by her example you shall be edified, by her prayers you shall be helped, by her admonitions you shall be inspired; you shall be inflamed with love; you shall rise higher in devotion; you shall be lifted up in meditation; you shall be filled with joy; you shall abound in consolation; you shall enjoy the things of heaven: from her lips you shall hear divine mysteries; you shall be taught things hidden from the world; you shall understand what others can only wonder at; you shall comprehend things unspeakable. By dwelling with her, you shall become more chaste than before; you shall remain altogether pure; you shall increase in holiness; you shall become more and more devout. Thanks be to God. **Amen.**

Jesus alone on the Cross

Matt. 27: 45-50

bless you, and give thanks to you, O Lord Jesus Christ, most loving Son of the Father's love, for your awful and lonely dereliction on the Cross. At the moment of your direst need – as if you had been an alien and of no account, as if you had not been the very Son of God and as if you had no power or merit of any kind soever – you were forsaken of God the Father, by the host of heaven, and by every creature upon earth. At this time your most sorrowful mother, attended only by a few poor women and by the disciple to whose care you had committed her, alone stood by you; and she, by reason of the grief and anguish of her soul, could scarce speak one word to you.

I praise and glorify you for that strong cry which burst from your lips, when in the hearing of all those that stood by, you uttered those woeful words: '*Eli, Eli, lamma sabachthani.*' By those words, O my Lord, you made abundantly plain the intensity of your anguish, and the withdrawal from you of consolation of every kind. You declared by them the measure of what you were enduring for the salvation of us men, by whom you were in return being set at nought, nay, rather, were being treated as the vilest of malefactors, and as one quite unworthy to live.

Mark well, O my soul, this word of Jesus; for it was spoken specially for your learning. Consider – Oh the wonder of it! – how the Lord of all things, who has need of nothing, is reduced to such a depth of misery that he tells forth his need into his Father's ears; that he who orders all things as co-worker with his Father, complains that his Father has forsaken him; that he who upholds all things by the word of his power proclaims the burden laid upon him to be too heavy for him to bear; that he, who is ever ready to comfort the mourner and the oppressed, confesses himself to be an outcast and forlorn; that he, who is the hearer of prayer, whose ears are ever open to the cry of the poor, humbly asks the question: 'My God, my God, why hast Thou forsaken Me?' Of a truth, from the beginning of his Passion until now, no words so woeful had yet been spoken.

It was for me, O Christ – I know it well – it was for me that in your passible human nature you uttered this cry upon the Cross; for your dereliction is my comfort; your bitter cry is my support; your weakness is my strength; your sufferings have paid the penalty for all my sins and shortcomings. You are the heavenly physician; moved by your infinite love and compassion, you submitted to be overwhelmed by unfathomable sorrow and anguish; and thus it is that with the weak you can be weak, with the mourner you can mourn, with the sinner you can be sad, with the oppressed you can grieve, and for all your weak members you can offer up prayer with strong crying and with tears. Those words which you uttered were not spoken by way of rebellion or of despair: they were the cry of your human nature and sensibility. Your flesh was suffering the penalty of guilt, of which it had never known the taint. Your divine nature brought no relief to your anguish; but it worked a miracle in your power of endurance, so that for the redemption of our race nothing might be wanting.

What faithful soul is there, which, after meditating on these things, can help sharing your anguish? What heart is there so hard as not to be pierced by that exceeding bitter cry? Even the elements, devoid of feeling as they are, stood unmistakably aghast in sympathy with your sufferings; for from the sixth until the ninth hour the sun withdrew its light from the world, refusing to shine upon men who were so unworthy of it . . .

Here, then, O disciple, is instruction for you, from the mouth of Jesus; he shows you what you should do when you are in distress. Are you suffering from some bodily infirmity? Have you some mental trouble or unhappiness to bear? Are you looked down upon by others? Have you lost the favour of men by reason of your poverty or other defect? Be not cast down, be not impatient; but use your trouble as a stepping-stone in your spiritual progress; use it as an oppourtunity for sweet converse with Jesus as he hangs upon the Cross, despised and rejected of men, and with the Father's face hidden from him for a season; and meditate upon those words which he spoke: 'My God, my God, why hast Thou forsaken Me?' **Amen.**

Jesus is thirsty

John 19: 28-29

I bless you, and give thanks to you, O Lord Jesus Christ, fountain of living water, and source of that wisdom that makes salvation known, for the exceeding great thirst which you suffered upon the Cross, because your sacred and precious blood had been poured forth, and all the natural fluids of your body had been exhausted by your grievous tortures. Besides your burning thirst for our salvation you endured an agony of bodily thirst; and as one utterly poor and needy, asked for a drink, saying, 'I thirst.' But there was none who would heed even this small request, none was there who would even offer a cup of water to him who made all water to flow. Nay more, some of the bystanders, on hearing what you had said, were not only not moved to pity, but became yet more unmerciful; and that they might gratify the hatred of their wicked hearts, filled a sponge with vinegar mingled with gall, and put to your sweet mouth that most bitter draught, which was not fit to be given as drink to a dog.

I laud and honour you for your most gracious self-restraint in accepting and tasting that most nauseous draught, which by way of expiatory penance for the sin of our first parents, you tasted in order that as the tasting of the forbidden fruit brought death into the world, so your tasting of this bitter draught might be to us a healing remedy.

Drink deeply, O disciple of Jesus, from this bitter cup as a cure for the indulgence of your appetites; for if you would sup with Christ in the kingdom of his Father, your heart must not be set upon dainty food, or draughts of costly wine; you must not long for soft beds or fine clothes. Such things are out of keeping with the spotless life of Jesus, and with his most bitter Passion. Be on your guard against yielding to the lusts of the flesh; keep your sensual impulses in check by being moderate in your food; and if you should exceed by taking too much or too dainty food, then by daily toil and nightly vigil chasten yourself for your fault, keeping ever sorrowfully in mind the bitter cup of Christ.

O Jesus, heavenly manna, and most sweet nectar, to whom vinegar and gall were given to drink when you were grievously athirst in your agony on the Cross; nor would anyone give you even a drop of water, by which you might have been refreshed; grant that at my meals I may be careful to remember this bitter cup of yours, so that I may not be too anxious about bodily nourishment, but may earnestly apply my mind to the holy words which are being read by a brother. May I learn to take only so much food as is needful for me; may I take it reverently, and may I devoutly thank you for all your benefits bestowed upon me.

May I be content, and that not grudgingly, with the food set before me, no matter how scanty or uninviting it may be: nay more, may I feel myself unworthy of even the poorest scraps and shrink from living in idleness at the cost of other men's labours. Grant that I may hunger after the meat that perishes not, but endures unto everlasting life. Grant that I may thirst after the fountain of life eternal, and that I may from time to time be fed with a crumb of that living bread which is set before those who eat at your table in heaven, and may be allowed to taste, be it ever so little, of its inward savour; so that I may be able experimentally to understand how refreshing is that Spirit, O Lord, which you shed forth upon the children of grace as a free gift. **Amen.**

The Scriptures are fulfilled

John 19:30

bless you, and give thanks to you, O Lord Jesus Christ, revealer of hidden mysteries, and fulfiller of the Law and the Prophets, for your most perfect accomplishment of the Father's will in that short and welcome word with which, as soon as you had received the vinegar, you closed, as it were, the story of your life by saying: 'It is finished.' This was as if you had openly said: 'Now is fulfilled all that the old Law foretold concerning me, all that was prefigured by the sacrificial rites and by the ceremonies of the former dispensation. Now are actually brought to pass the inspired words of the holy prophets, and the long-cherished desires of the patriarchs. Now is all that is needed for the redemption of the human race fully worked out; now has been accomplished in a perfect way, both as to place and time, all that Holy Scripture has recorded of the promises of God. The few things that remain will surely in due time be made good. I have fulfilled my Father's command: he sent me into the world; and I have finished the work which he gave me to do.

'Many a time and often have I healed the sick; I have given abundant proofs of my divine power; as the Father has taught me so have I spoken in the world, and no part of saving doctrine have I kept back from the ears of the faithful. For three and thirty years have I been a pilgrim upon earth, and have dwelt as a friend among men; many a time and often have I been wearied by journeyings: cruelly have I been slandered by my enemies; I have been betrayed by one of my disciples; I have been deserted by my friends; I have been held captive by my enemies, and have been scourged by their underlings; I have been condemned by judges, and mocked by chief priests; and now, guiltless as I am, I am hanging here upon the Cross. What is there that I ought to have done more than I have done? What ought I to have suffered that I have not suffered? If I have failed in doing or in suffering anything, I am ready before my departure to make it good: but no, by my death, I shall satisfy to the last penny every debt. To-day, therefore, do I pronounce all to be accomplished. Nor do I allow the term of my life to be further prolonged; but I lay down my life for my sheep, out of pure love for them.

'At this hour, which I know to be the same as that in which the first Adam, by taking of the forbidden tree, incurred the penalty of eternal death, I take upon myself, of my own free choice, in satisfaction of the debt due by sinners for their sins, the penalty of the death of my body, a penalty to which I am not liable for any sin of my own. The things concerning me shall shortly have an end. Henceforth I shall not speak much in this world: I shall not long be in it, because I haste to the Father. Toil shall now cease, sorrow and mourning shall flee away, fighting shall have an end, trouble shall be no more, and at my death, death itself shall be destroyed: nothing more remains to be done, except that I should commend my spirit to my Father, and should quit my body until the third day.'

O Jesus Christ, who order all things in heaven and in earth, who are the brightest and most perfect model of every virtue, and the endless reward of every good work, direct, I pray you, all my actions in the way of your commandments, and purify and enlighten every thought of my mind. Teach me to begin, humbly and with an eye to the praise and glory of your blessed name, every work which I undertake; to be diligent in performing it, and to bring it to a happy end. Grant that I may not grow slack before the time appointed of the Father; but that until I breathe my last breath, I may labour night and day and may work my very hardest in the workshop of our heavenly Father's business; so that, after many a struggle and much hard toil, I may at length, when my last hour shall come, be able by your mercy joyfully to say with you: 'It is finished.' **Amen**.

LENT 31

Jesus departs

Luke 23: 46-49

 bless you, and give thanks to you, O Lord Jesus Christ, life of the living, hope of the dying, Saviour of all who trust in you, for your departure for a season out of this world; and for your happy return, through the agony of a cruel death, and the splendid martyrdom of the Cross, to the bosom of the Father.

I praise and glorify you for your ashy paleness at the moment of death, for your sacred last agony, for the gradual failure of your bodily powers, and for the breaking of your heart so full of love – all which was the penalty which, as the giver of life to all things that have breath, you did not shrink from paying, when you submitted yourself to the sentence of death, in order that thereby you might open to us the way to the kingdom of heaven.

I praise and glorify you for the loud cry which you uttered from the Cross with superhuman strength; for the sad divorce and bitter parting of your all-glorious soul from your body so full of love; for the most devout commendation of your soul into the Father's hands; for the meek bowing of your sacred and thorn-crowned head upon your breast, in token of filial obedience persisted in to the last; for your loving yielding-up of your all-holy soul for the salvation of the world; and for that cry of loving prayer, saying: 'Father, into Thy Hands I commend my Spirit' – which done, you straightway drew your last breath, and falling into a calm sleep, brought your earthly sojourn to an end.

And now, O my soul, see how the holy and righteous One dies, and no man lays it to heart: no one, save his poor sorrowful mother (who, with a scanty following of her friends, realizes who, and how mighty, he was). Stand, then, by Mary's side, and meditate with a sad heart upon the death of Jesus.

Jesus, who had done no wrong to any man, dies naked and as a slave; nowhere could anyone be found in a worse case than his. No one was ever so dear to God, and yet no one was ever more despised of men, than was Jesus of Nazareth. See how the world repaid him for all the mighty works and wonders he had wrought in it. He is put to death as if he were the vilest of robbers; he dies as if he were the poorest of men. The deathbed of Jesus is not of down, but is the hard wood of the Cross: he dies with no house or even roof to cover him, but in the open air, on a spot loathsome and disgusting; not in a private chamber, but at the place of public execution; not surrounded by his disciples, but between two thieves; not in his mother's embrace, but nailed to the arms of a lofty Cross.

Beneath him he had not even a bundle of straw; to cover him, he had not even a piece of the cheapest sackcloth. No pillow had he for his head; but there was given him instead a wreath of sharp thorns. No shoes had he for his feet, or gloves for his hands; but instead of these, iron nails driven through both hands and feet, piercing both flesh and bones. In his supreme need he had not even one attendant; but he had to tolerate instead a loathsome companion – an impenitent thief, who all the while was blaspheming him. Not only had he no comforter, but he was forsaken by almost all those who had once been his followers and familiar friends. He could move neither hand nor foot, nor was he able to relieve his pain by turning from side to side.

There he hangs nailed fast to his Cross, stretched out till he can be stretched no further, tortured to the limit of endurance, racked in every limb, with no one to care for him, no one to help him, no one to comfort him, heartbroken. His tongue was all that was left him free to use; and he used it in praying for his enemies, and in preaching to us from the pulpit of the Cross his seven most wholesome Words against the seven deadly sins. But even his tongue was not left without its torments; for when he was athirst it was steeped in gall and vinegar. From the soles of his feet therefore to the top of his head, Jesus is overwhelmed in the sea of his Passion; and about the ninth hour he cries out with a loud voice, and dies. Thanks be to God. **Amen**.

Words from the Cross

Luke 23:34; 23:43; John 19: 26-27; Matt. 27:46;
John 19:28; 19:30; Luke 23:46

all to mind, O my soul, the seven Words of Jesus, which he spoke from the Cross for your instruction.

As soon as he had been raised upon his Cross, he prayed for his enemies, and forgave those who were illtreating him; and this he did in order that you might learn to forgive from the heart those who have wronged you, before you plead for your own forgiveness.

Next, he promised to the penitent thief the joys of Paradise; and this he did in order that you should not despair by reason of the grievous burden of your sins; but should, with full trust in his mercy, ask him to remember you in the kingdom of heaven.

Thirdly, he committed his most blessed mother to the chaste John; and this he did in order that you, in your agony, should confidently have recourse to Mary, his most gentle mother, who is the helper of those who are in need, and should earnestly commend yourself to her, and to the blessed apostle John, and to all the saints. Commend yourself also to the prayers of your brethren, and to those of all the faithful, asking them to remember you.

Fourthly, Jesus made it plain that he was left alone in his anguish; and this he did in order that, when you have a heavy burden of pain to bear, you should not be impatient at not immediately finding relief from it, but should submit yourself in all things to God's holy will and pleasure.

Fifthly, he said 'I thirst,' in order that you should have a burning thirst after God, who is the fountain of living water, and should long to depart, and to be with Christ; for this is far better than to prolong your sojourn upon earth, and to be further exposed to dangers of every kind.

Sixthly, he declared: 'It is finished,' in order that, when you perceive your last hour to be at hand, you should render thanks to God for every good action of your life, and should pray that your shortcomings may be supplied by the merits of Christ.

Lastly, with a loud voice he commended his soul into the Father's hands, in order that at the hour of your departure from the world you too should not fail to have upon your tongue, and often to repeat, the words of that blessed commendation. You cannot find anything more sweet to be remembered at the last than that.

O most loving Jesus, brightness of the Father's glory, and sun of righteousness, who for me, your poor unworthy servant, vouchsafed to suffer this most shameful form of agony; and when delivering up your soul upon the hill of Calvary, for the redemption of the world, commended it in prayer to the Father, grant that I may ever feel within me both sorrow and love for your most cruel death; grant that, by mortifying all my corrupt affections, I may daily exercise myself in dying with you; so that when the hour of my departure shall be at hand, I may be found meet to live again in the light of your mercies, and joyfully to enter with you, into the bliss of Paradise.

Stand by my deathbed, help me in my agony, come to me when I need you most, defend me from my enemies, deliver me from my distress; comfort me in my sorrow, strengthen me when I am dismayed, refresh me when I faint, take me to yourself when my last sigh is breathed. May your last Word upon the Cross be my last word on earth; and when speech fails me, give heed to this last wish of my soul: 'Father, into Thy Hands I commend my spirit: Thou has redeemed me, O Lord, the God of Truth.'   **Amen**.

LENT 33

Jesus's body is pierced

John 19: 31-35

 bless you, and give thanks to you, O Lord Jesus Christ, exhaustless fount of love and grace, for the cruel piercing after death of your most holy side. So fiercely was your right side struck and pierced by the lance of one of the soldiers, that the weapon, passing through your inward parts, entered your tender heart, and from the gaping wound thus made there came forth a fountain of blood and water, so wholesome for us, that, sprinkled with it, all mankind may be healed.

O wondrous fountain of the holy blood welling out from the right side of Christ as he hung in death upon the Cross, flowing ever onward for the redemption of the human race! O bright and most refreshing stream of blessed water gushing forth from the Saviour's heart for the washing away of all our sins! Under the old covenant, Moses, the servant of the Lord, smote the rock in the wilderness, and there came forth so plenteous a supply of water that the people and their cattle drank thereof with joy, and no longer murmured.

But the brawny soldier, Longinus, when he opened Christ's right side, struck the Rock with his lance so fierce a blow, that from it blood and water have never ceased to pour; and our holy Mother, the Church, has drawn from there the sacraments, by means of which her life is preserved: for as Eve is called the mother of all living, and was formed from her husband Adam's rib, so is the holy Church militant named the Mother of all the faithful, and she is the new creation from the side of Christ, her Spouse.

O mighty and precious wound of my Lord, worthy of love are you above all wounds; so deep and so wide are you that all the faithful may enter by you into the side of Christ; miraculous are you in what flows from you; most copious in blessings; in time last formed, in glory preeminent. Of the divine and holy fountain of this wound whosoever shall drink, or of its love taste but one drop, he shall forget all his evil deeds, shall be cured of the fever of carnal and worldly desires, shall burn with love for the things which are eternal, shall be filled with the joy unspeakable of the Holy Spirit; and this holy fountain shall become in him a fountain of living water springing up unto everlasting life.

Go in, go in, my soul, into the right side of your crucified Lord! Enter through that glorious wound into the most loving heart of Jesus, pierced with the lance for love of you, so that in the cleft of that Rock you may take refuge from the tempest of the world! Draw near, O man, to that heart so exalted, but made so low for you; to the heart of God, who is so far above you, but who opens to you his door! Come in, you blessed of the Lord; why do you stand without? The river of life, the way of salvation, the heavenly storehouse, shedding perfumes all around; all these lie open to you. Here is a place of refuge from the face of the enemy who would tempt you; here is a place in which you may find mercy against the wrath of the judgement to come.

Here is a fountain, whence the oil of gladness and of grace shall never cease to flow, wherein sinners may ever find mercy, if only they will come to it with hearts truly penitent and contrite. Here is the well-spring of the river of God, going forth from the midst of Paradise to water the face of the earth, to give the thirsty soul to drink, to wash away sins, to quench the flames of lust, to still the strivings of anger. Do not hesitate to drink from this fountain of the Saviour a cup of love. Take from the side of Jesus sweet helps for your life, that henceforth you may live not in yourself, but in him who was wounded for you.

Give your heart to him, who has opened his to you. Enter through the hallowed wound into the inmost heart of your Redeemer. He bids you enter; he asks you to dwell with him; his wish is that you should have but one heart with him. 'My son,' he says to you, 'give Me thy heart.' This is all that God asks of you: give but this, and you have offered the gift most acceptable to him. Give it, then, to Jesus, and to none else besides: give it to Christ, and not to the world. **Amen**.

The wounds of Jesus

John 19: 31-35

esus Christ caused his side to be thrown so widely open, and to be so deeply pierced, in order that the way by which you might draw near to the heart of your Beloved should be made plain to you; in order that you might penetrate into the very soul of the Son of God, and be made one with him in true union of heart; that you might centre all your affections upon him, and might, in singleness of heart, do all your works to his honour and glory; that you might study to please him alone, and might strive with all your mind and with all your strength to serve him, and him only.

Where can you rest more securely, where dwell more safely, where sleep your last sleep more sweetly, than in the wounds of Jesus Christ, who suffered for you, from out of whose breast there is ever flowing for your use a stream of living water? Where, when your love is beginning to grow cold, can it be more powerfully rekindled? Where can you so readily avoid distraction? Where can you be kept so fully recollected, as in the heart of Jesus, which for love of you was pierced with the lance? Nothing inflames, nothing draws, nothing gets to the bottom of the heart of man so thoroughly as love for the crucified Redeemer.

It was this thought which led Ignatius of Antioch to exclaim: 'My love was crucified.' To which with all my heart I echo: 'My love was wounded and pierced, so that I might find a ready entrance into his loving heart.'

To it, then, make all the eager loving haste which you can make bold to show; kiss the holy side of Jesus, so that you may be sprinkled with water and with blood from there. Pull out your own heart, if you can, and place it close to the heart of Jesus, in order that he may keep it, and rule it, and possess it, so that other things may not get hold of it, and defile it. Open you heart to him; commit yourself in full trust to him; leave to him your 'I will' and 'I won't'; let there be one heart and one mind between you and God: so that you may think and feel with him in all things, and may know his holy will both now and evermore. When without reserve you shall have made over your heart to Jesus, for him to keep and to dwell therein for ever, then shall great peace be yours, nor shall you be easily put out, or distressed by the troubles of your daily life.

O most pure Jesus, who dwells in the hearts of those who love you, and from whom all good desires do come; O you, who hang upon the Cross before the eyes of all who meditate upon your Passion; O divine treasure-house of all gifts and graces; O Christ my King, Redeemer of the faithful, who caused your most holy side to be pierced by the point of a cruel lance; set open for me, I beseech you, the door of your mercy; suffer me to enter through the gaping wound of your side into the very recesses of your most loving heart; so that my heart may be set on fire by your touch, and may be united to you by a bond of love so indissoluble, that you may dwell in me, and I in you, and that nothing may ever separate me from you.

Pierce my heart with the arrow of your love, may the soldier's spear pass through me, and penetrate the inmost recesses of my heart, so that, by means of this wholesome wound, my soul may attain perfect health. May I refuse all love but yours and seek comfort nowhere else but only in you. May my heart be free of access and lie open to you alone; may it be estranged from the world, shut to the devil, and fenced on all sides by the sign of the Cross to resist temptation of every kind.   **Amen**.

The dead body of Jesus

John 19: 36-37

bless you, and give thanks to you, O Lord Jesus Christ, spotless mirror of the majesty of God, for the pale and piteous appearance, due to death's onset, which you presented, when after your soul had left your body, evident signs of mortality showed themselves in you.

Alas, alas, my Jesus, fairest of men, the comeliness of your pleasant countenance has been marred by the filthy spitting upon you of men of unclean lips, and in your contest with death you have lost the bloom of your beauteous manhood! Alas, my most loving God, all these things have befallen you because my sins had to be washed away: it was in order that my soul might be made white, that you submitted your body to be made unsightly; it was to save me from eternal death, that you tasted for a while the most cruel of deaths. O death, what have you done? How is it that you were not afraid to lay your hand upon the Lord's Anointed? What power had you over him; what crime could you lay to the charge of the Son of God? You have fallen upon him, and slain him; but your victory has cost you dear: for in slaying him you have slain yourself; impaled upon the stake of Christ's divinity, you have brought to an end your cruel reign.

Come then, O faithful soul, and look upon the pale and careworn features of your crucified Saviour; mark each several limb of Jesus who is dead, and let the greatness of your compassion make your eyes run down with tears. Your time is well spent, very sacred are your thoughts, when you are occupied in contemplating Jesus hanging on the Cross.

There before you is the tree of the Cross, upon which hangs your Salvation; of the devout the Redemption, of unbelievers the laughing-stock. His lifeless, thorn-crowned head is bowed low upon his sacred breast. The eyes of him from whose all-seeing eye no secret can be hid, are sightless now. The ears of him who foreknows all things, hear nothing now. He who gives to flowers the sweetness of their scent, smells nothing now. The sense of taste has gone from him who gives to all things that have life their life and food. He who makes the dumb to speak opens his lips no more. He who teaches men knowledge is silent now. That tongue which preached the truth lies useless in his throat. That face, which once was brighter than the sun, is now deadly pale. Those cheeks, which once were fair as a turtle-dove's, are fair no longer. Those hands, by which the heavens were spread out, are pierced now with cruel nails. The knees, so often bent in prayer, hang now limp and powerless. The legs, which like marble pillars used to support the body's weight, have now lost all their strength. The feet, which were so often weary when the gospel was being preached, are now as tightly fastened to the wood of the Cross as if they were fixed in the stocks. It can be seen that every limb has been in agony; they are each one covered with wounds and blood.

But his bones are not broken, as are the bones of the thieves: and this is in order that the Scripture might be fulfilled; for he is the true Lamb, prefigured in the Law, the bones of which were ordered to be kept unbroken. This is my Beloved, O daughters of Jerusalem. This is my friend; and it is to this condition that death has brought him, in exchange for whose death – so precious was he – if I could submit to a thousand deaths, I could make no due return for his love.

O most sweet Jesus, Redeemer of my soul, how can I win to die with you upon the Cross; how, at my departure from the body, can I obtain such happiness? Grant, I earnestly beseech you, that in this frail body I may so live, so order all my doings and all my affections in accordance with your will, that I may be able to finish my course in a state of grace; and in spite of all the temptations which beset me, may receive at last the crown of joy eternal. **Amen**.

Jesus is taken down

John 19: 38-42

bless you, and give thanks to you, O Lord Jesus Christ, power of God, for your lowly descent (at the hour of Vespers) from the lofty Cross, upon which, for our Salvation, you hung till sunset. You were then ordered to be taken down from it in accordance with the Jewish law, and because the Paschal Feast was about to be kept on Holy Saturday.

I praise and glorify you for the faithful service so lovingly rendered you by your familiar friends. Those most just men, Joseph of Arimathea, and Nicodemus, a Doctor of the Law, came with their servants to the Cross, and having set up ladders against it, mounted one on the right and another on the left, while a third was engaged in loosing your feet. With due reverence and love, they drew from your sacred hands and feet three precious nails, more precious than burnished gold; and then with the help of their companions, they reverently took hold of your most illustrious body, and modestly and carefully lowered it to the ground.

Blessed and full of pity were you men, who did this act of mercy to the Lord your God, in order to prepare his body for the grave; you were careful to show even more faithful devotion to your friend when he was dead than you had shown to him when he was alive. Therefore, in heaven shall you receive a special reward from God, to whom you showed yourselves so faithful upon earth: and without doubt he for whom you prepared a burial place upon earth will reward your loving care by preparing for you a happy mansion in heaven, as on the night before his death he promised his disciples.

Oh that to me too, the least of all God's servants, might have been granted some share in the burial of my Lord; that in the offices connected with it, some service, however small, might have been assigned to me! How willingly would I have held the ladder at the Cross's foot; or, as I stood below, have handed up the pincers for the drawing of the nails; or even lent a helping hand to those who were lowering the sacred corpse. What happiness would it have been if I could have stood beneath the Cross, so close to it as to have caught in my bosom one of the falling nails, which I might have kept as a memorial of my Lord's Passion, so that whenever I should look upon it, I might be moved to tears.

I praise and glorify you for that longing embrace with which your most sorrowful mother received you into her arms, and folded you therein, when with compassionate devotion your faithful ones delivered you to her, and laid you in her lap. How copious were the tears that then streamed from those eyes, of all eyes the purest; how burning was the flood that then bedewed that face, of all faces the most modest, and fell from your mother's cheeks upon your corpse! How pure were the kisses with which your chaste mother then covered your lifeless limbs; how often, and with what anguish, did she examine the prints of your sacred wounds. How loving were the arms with which she encircled and held the blessed fruit of her womb, that fruit which she had seen sacrificed upon the altar of the Cross for the redemption of mankind! Who is there among the saints who could tell forth the copiousness of those tears which the tender mother of Jesus at that time shed, or could understand the full agony of her grief?

Draw near, then, now my soul, and devoutly kiss the blood-red wounds of Jesus. As he hung nailed to the Cross you could not come near to him for the pressure of the crowd and the height of the Cross; but now he lies before you in his weeping mother's arms, dead and covered with wounds. Draw near, O sinner, however great your sinfulness, however much the fear of hell oppresses you; for it was for you that the Lamb was slain; it was for you that the Victim was offered, which has taken away the sin of all the world. So loving and merciful is the Lord Jesus, so tender and so sweet is Mary his mother, that none can depart uncomforted, none go away empty, who with his whole heart shall have asked to be forgiven.   **Amen**.

Prayers to Jesus

To the Feet

beauteous feet of my Lord Jesus Christ, which were transfixed by one most cruel nail being driven through you both, and from which came forth much precious blood, I reverently adore you; and I kiss you, earnestly praying that the sins which I have committed in standing or walking may be forgiven me.

To the Legs

O beauteous legs, and humble knees of my Lord Jesus Christ, which were in prayer so often bent and prostrate upon the naked earth, which were racked with burning fever in his Passion, I humbly adore you; and I kiss you, meekly entreating that the sins which I have so often committed by my lack of fervour and devotion in the service of God may mercifully be forgiven me.

To the Side

O most adorable side of my Lord Jesus Christ, in which the wound of divine Love is to be seen pierced through and through, I specially adore you; and I cover you with kisses, earnestly imploring that the sins which I have so often committed against brotherly charity, and by waxing cold in my love for God, may be forgiven me.

To the Back

O most patient back of my Lord Jesus Christ, which was ready without a murmur to bear the tree of Life, and the burden of the sins of all sinners, which also submitted to be most cruelly scourged, I devoutly adore you; and I reverently kiss you, praying that the sins which I have committed by being impatient under the burdens laid upon me may be forgiven me.

To the Hands

O adorable hands of my Lord Jesus Christ, which were stretched out to their widest upon the Cross, and were pierced by great iron nails, I devoutly adore you; and with tears in my eyes I kiss you, and pray that all the sins which I have committed by act, or by touch, may be done away.

To the Mouth

O most sweet mouth of my Lord Jesus Christ, out of which the word of salvation went forth into the world, which was defiled by the spittle of the Jews, and which was embittered with the draught of vinegar, I adore you; and I gently kiss you, entreating that the sins which I have so often committed in eating, drinking, and speaking may be forgiven me.

To the Face

O illustrious face of my Lord Jesus Christ, full of kindliness and awe, which was so foully spat upon by the Jews, which was so shamefully buffeted, and mockingly veiled, I adore you with the reverence which is your due; and I lovingly kiss you, praying you to pardon me all the disrespect by which I have so many times given offence to your Majesty.

To the Eyes

O eyes of my Lord Jesus Christ, brightly shining, never soiled by any evil desire, now dimmed by death; eyes from which many a time came forth a shower of tears, with all my heart I adore you; and I gently kiss you, praying the while for pardon for all the stains upon my soul caused by sight used unlawfully.

To the Head

O sublime and adorable head of my Lord Jesus Christ, having now a sharp crown of thorns pressed down upon the top of you, and your hair stained and hallowed by the blood which has run down upon you, I join the angels and all the heavenly host in adoring you; upon each of your sacred wounds I print loving kisses; and I earnestly entreat you to rid me from all the thorn-pricks which my sins have left in me, and to vouchsafe to number me among your elect, even though my place must needs be found among the least of all the members of your body. **Amen**

Jesus washes their feet

John 13: 1-17

bless you, and give thanks to you, O Lord Jesus Christ, most highly exalted King of saints, for that supreme example of deep humility and abject self-abasement, which you showed forth, and left to us for our imitation. You, the most holy God, thought no scorn of carefully washing, on your bended knees, and with your own ever-blessed hands, of wiping, and of kissing, the feet of those poor fishermen, your humble followers: and, more than all this, you also washed, with the same tender loving-kindness, the feet of your unfaithful betrayer, although, ungrateful for all your benefits, foul within and unwashed, he went on still in his wickedness.

I praise and glorify you for your long reclining at the table of this most sacred Last Supper, at which you performed so many wondrous acts of love, that time would fail for their worthy recital.

I praise and glorify you, O Jesus, of comforters the best, of teachers the sweetest, of helpers the most powerful, for that long, notable, and heavenly discourse, full of the fire of love and sweet as a honey-comb, which you delivered to your disciples (John 13-17) in words which all might understand, after the washing of the feet and the departure of the traitor Judas. By it you took pains to comfort and strengthen their sad hearts against the tribulations which were to come upon them, giving them a sure hope of your resurrection, of their being strengthened by the coming of the Holy Spirit, and of their being received after this their exile into the heavenly mansions of your Father; adding moreover many most beautiful words. And at last, at the close of this sacred utterance, with a faithfulness that knew no bounds, you did, in true union of heart, gather them all up in your commendation of them to God the Father, saying: 'O Father, I will that they may be all one, as we also are.'

I pray you now, O most loving Jesus, my Master and my Lord, that you would grant to me who am the chiefest of sinners, and your unworthy servant, to meditate with recollected mind upon your words so heavenly, and upon your doings so vividly set forth. Grant to me especially, I beseech you, to bow my most stubborn of necks to the doing of all work, no matter how humble, and to the fulfilment of all duties, no matter how servile; utterly to overcome my pride and false shame, so that I may learn to spend myself in the loving service, not only of my friends, but also of those who are repulsive to me from defects of mind or body. May I never think it a great matter to have to ask pardon for my shortcomings, when you, my God, were not ashamed to bend your most sacred knees in the presence of your disciples, and to wash their feet. Taught, as I am, by your example, help me to carry into act what I hear and read of you.

But because I am at all points full of faults, and stained with all kinds of evil propensities, I need to be cleansed from my sins by a washing of exceeding thoroughness. To you, therefore, do I stretch forth my hands; and with the knees of my heart humbly bent before you, I pray that you would vouchsafe to wash carefully and thoroughly, not my feet only, but also my hands and my head; for in many ways have I sinned against you, by thought and by speech, both in what I have done and in what I have left undone.

Wash me, therefore, O my Jesus, from all the filth of my sins, cleanse me from every defilement, whether of body or of soul; so that, being made clean from head to foot, I may be found meet to have part with you, in that everlasting joy, which you have promised to all your loved ones, who in times of temptation have held fast to you.

Give me also, I pray you, an understanding heart, that I may be able fully to comprehend that most sweet discourse, which you spoke at the Supper: for its words are indeed words breathing most fervent love, the sweetest comfort, and the most exalted wisdom. So write your new commandment upon the tables of my heart, that my soul may be on fire with the twofold love which it enjoins: strengthen me in every trouble that may come upon me, and in place of this world's joys, fill me with the most sweet comfort of your Holy Spirit. **Amen**.

GOOD FRIDAY

Jesus is buried

John 19: 38-42

Lord Jesus Christ, sweet savour of life, and brightness of the everlasting day, I bless you, and give thanks to you for the careful preparing with precious spices of your sacred body for its burial. This was not indeed needful for warding off corruption; but you accepted it as showing the devotion of your friends, and as being in accordance with Jewish custom – witness the instances of like burial recorded of certain of the patriarchs and kings.

I praise and glorify you, for the loving enwrapment of your sacred body in a clean linen cloth, and for the respectful binding round of your ever-blessed head with a pure white napkin, which was afterwards found in the holy sepulchre.

I praise and glorify you for the removal, amid many tears, of your body to the place of its burial; for the reverence with which it was placed there; for your condescension in lying in the new tomb hewn out of a rock, which was provided for you by Joseph, a noble counsellor; where, because the hour was late, you were honourably buried by your weeping friends, and your tomb was tightly closed up with a heavy stone.

Learn too, O my soul, from the burial of Jesus to meditate with profit upon the dissolution of your own body. That which you received from the earth, that to the earth you must restore: dust you are and to dust shall you return. Upon what then do you pride yourself, you who must soon decompose and be hidden out of sight

76

in the ground? What do you see to yearn after in a world, out of which you must so soon be cast, trodden under foot of men? Whenever then you look upon the graves of the dead, remember that you too will soon be with them. There – and you know it well – there is the home appointed for every one that lives.

There, laid low together, content with a mere corner of earth, shall the rich man and the poor man share one bed. There gentleman and commoner cannot be known the one from the other, and the strong and the weak are upon the same footing. There the miser's wealth will not profit him; nor will the crafty man be helped by all his cunning. There the pleasure-seeking will be food for worms, and the vain man will stink in the nostrils of the passer-by. There the loftiness of men will be bowed down, and the counsel of the haughty ones will be brought to nothing. Remember that nothing mortal can endure for ever, and that man, having corrupted his nature by sin, must needs go back to the slime from which he was taken.

Strive so to live in this present world, and so to mortify by the Spirit the deeds of the flesh, that when your body is mouldering in the dust your soul may be found meet to rest in a home of blessed peace. Spend the Good Friday of this life in painfulness and toil, and you shall have a Holy Saturday of rest, and an Easter of joy unspeakable at the resurrection of the just. The stricter therefore your life in this world, the calmer shall be your sleep in the tomb; the stronger now your hold upon the Cross, the greater shall be your confidence when you come into the presence of Christ.

Bewail then, bewail now your sins, while the day of grace is yours, while the door of mercy stands open, while God, with whom is plenteous redemption, is ready to accept your penitence. Bewail also the unhappy condition of the world, and that grievous softness of men, as a result of which so few true followers of the Crucified are to be found, and that the spritual fervour of so many soon grows cold.

Henceforth, then, be it your daily practice to meditate upon Christ Jesus. Him crucified keep ever before your eyes; stand ever beneath your Saviour's Cross; in life and in death be with Jesus in the tomb; so that when Christ, my Life, shall appear, you too may rise with him in glory. **Amen**.

HOLY SATURDAY

Jesus descends into Hades

 praise and honour you, O most gracious Jesus, for mercifully visiting in Limbo the saints of the old dispensation, and for releasing all the faithful souls which were resting in Abraham's bosom. They indeed had for a long time anxiously looked for your descent into Hades, and with eyes full of tears were lovingly exclaiming, as we do now in this day's processional: 'Thou art come, O loved One, whom we have long waited for in our darkness; Thou art this night come to bring forth from the prison house those who were bound.'

Lead, then, the chorus of joy, O Adam, our first parent, founder, so far as man can be said so to be, of the human race; rejoice together with Eve, your wife of high renown, formed from your side in Paradise! Rejoice; for Christ, a descendant of your own, virgin-born, and sacrificed upon the Cross, has come to deliver you and all your fellow-captive descendants, who have died trusting in him, and in the hope of heavenly grace! Christ has come to deliver you from the power of the grave, out of the house of bondage, out of the shadow of death, out of the den of lions, from the fear of the evil demons; and to bring you and all the saints of whom you were the ancestors, attended by the angels who were your dear companions when on earth, amid songs of sweet rejoicing, into a Paradise of delight and of everlasting bliss.

You too rejoice, O holy patriarch Abraham, father of many nations; rejoice with Sarah, your faithful wife, over the Incarnation of Christ, foretold to you, and crowned with this Festival! This is the day which you had long expected, and wished to see. Firmly you believed and therefore you have been found worthy to be made glad by beholding with your own eyes Christ, born of your seed, the giver of the kingdom of heaven.

You too rejoice, most ancient father Isaac, at the bright vision of Christ, and at his descent into Hades, concerning which, before your death you prophesied; and when blessing your son Jacob, you did in mysterious words beautifully point to Christ as of holy ones the most blessed, and did speak his praises in these words: 'Behold the smell of my son is as the smell of a plentiful field, which the Lord hath blessed. Cursed be he that curseth thee; and let him that blesseth thee be filled with blessings!'

You too rejoice over this day, O mighty wrestler Jacob, chiefly for the heavenly glory and the gracious glance of Jesus Christ. In days long past, when you were blessing your sons, you prophetically spoke in these words of faith and prayer: 'I will look for Thy salvation, O Lord!' O word truly sweet to the ear, and full of joy to the godly! O wholesome word, which in its inner meaning speaks of Jesus, long desired by patriarchs and prophets, patiently expected, and now at length shown forth before their eyes; for there is no other name under heaven given to men, whereby we must be saved, except this most sweet name of Jesus, which is blessed for ever above all things, from everlasting to everlasting!

Yes, in very truth, Jesus himself, the salvation of God promised in the Law, who was born of a virgin, who suffered on the Cross, who rose again on the third day, who fulfilled all things which the holy patriarchs and all the prophets had spoken concerning him. Speak then now quite plainly, O holy Jacob, in the joy of your heart; say of Christ appearing in the glory of his Father in the sight of the angels of God: 'I have seen my Lord face to face, and my soul has been saved!' What would you have more than this; and what greater happiness could you desire? If on seeing one of God's angels, your joy was so great, what ought now your joy to be when you have been found worthy to behold the Lord of angels?

O all holy patriarchs and prophets, O kings and rulers of the people, O young men and old, O virgins and faithful widows, O priests and Levites, O doctors and scribes, O spirits and souls of the just, O holy and humble men of heart, rejoice all this day and be glad in Jesus Christ our Lord, who has become our Salvation! Praise him and magnify him for ever; for he has himself come to visit you, and to bring joy to the hearts of all who were waiting for the redemption of his people Israel! **Amen**.

Twelve Meditations

for

Easter

The Victory of Jesus

Mark 8:31

bless you, and give thanks to you, O Lord Jesus Christ, for your victory and triumph upon the Cross over death, and for your glorious and joyful resurrection from the tomb, in which, after being buried amid many tears, you did, for our sakes, lie for three days and nights, actually a corpse, hidden from every human eye, and closed up with a great stone, so that you could neither be touched nor seen by your disciples or friends. You were, moreover, watched by a strong guard of heathen soldiers.

But in this case surely the wickedness of evil men recoiled upon themselves; and all craftiness of the devil, all the might of Pilate, all the wrong-headedness of the people, all the knavery of the priests, all the wisdom of the scribes, all the counsel of the Pharisees and of the elders – anxious to wipe out your holy name from among men – were brought to nought.

When therefore, O most merciful Lord Jesus, midnight was past, and dawn was at hand, in a glorious body, in an atmosphere of joy and unspeakable light, you rose happily again to life from the sealed tomb; even as at your birth you came forth from the womb of your most holy mother the virgin Mary, without breaking the seal of her perpetual virginity – a stupendous mystery, an unheard-of miracle, possible only because of the presence and power of the Holy Spirit.

And this is why you established the festival of the resurrection to be for ever kept most holy, as brighter than the sun and more glorious than all the festivals of the year; and provided that throughout the world it should be celebrated with joyful hearts and voices, in hymns and psalms, and with frequent Alleluias, and be most conspicuously honoured by joyous remembrance and thanksgiving by the faithful. **Amen.**

The visit to the tomb

Matt. 28: 1-10

praise and honour you, O most gracious Jesus, for your exceeding gentleness, and for the loving and comforting words with which you greeted the holy women when they met you in the way, allowing them to clasp your most sacred feet – those feet which were nailed to the Cross, which are brighter than the sun, whiter than snow, more precious than gold, sweeter smelling than any balm or chrism.

O Almighty Lord Jesus, I give you most hearty thanks for sending from heaven your holy angel to roll away the great stone from the sepulchre; to drive away the heathen guard from that holy place where you safely rested, as a strong lion in his den; to prepare for the men and for the women, who loved you, free access to the tomb; to comfort those who were bewailing you as dead and buried; to confirm and strengthen the halting faith of those who were doubting your resurrection; and to rejoice with you at your happy return from the descent into Hades, and at the setting open of the gate of heaven.

Grief at your crucifixion had taken such full possession of the hearts of those holy women, that they had quite given up hoping for your resurrection, in spite of your having so often foretold it. Nowhere could they have found comfort, had they not visited your sepulchre that morning; had they not heard from the mouth of the angel that in very truth you had risen; had they not in confirmation of the truth seen you with their own eyes and clasped with their own hands your glorious feet. But when all these things had been done, you added to the comfort you had given them by a loving greeting of them, and by laying upon them a joyful duty – a duty worthy of all acceptance and honour – lovingly consoling and encouraging them with the words: 'Fear not; go, tell my brethren that they go into Galiliee, there they shall see Me.'

How delightful are those words to the ear, how sweet are they to the mind, how profitable are they for meditation, and for taking the place of gossip about the things of this world! How bright must have been the eyes that had seen the Lord, how pure the hands that had touched Jesus, how holy the lips that had printed on him a kiss. How swift in walking and how quick in running must have been made the feet; how prompt in obedience must have been made the hearts; how joyful must have been made the lips of those who were bidden to tell the disciples that the Lord was risen. Great as was that Good Friday burden of sorrows when the ignominious cross of Jesus was seen upon the hill of Calvary, out of all proportion greater far must have been the joys of that first Easter Day, when the glorious tidings of the resurrection were made known. The reproach of the Jews is turned into the exceeding great joy of the apostles; the offence of the Cross has become the means of everlasting salvation; the tears of the saints have given place to the songs of angels; and the wounds made by the scourging and the nails have won for us the remission of our sins.

O most sweet Jesus Christ, kindle also in my heart, I pray you, the love of your holy name, so that, with Mary Magdalene and her companions, I may remember it every morning at the break of day, and may seek you in the sepulchre of my heart; may be utterly dead to the things of this world, and may cling devoutly to you in the silence and the solitude of prayer. Keep my heart from being hard, my body from being slothful, my eyes from being drowsy. Give me the grace of true contrition, fill me with the joy of true devotion, so that I may worthily celebrate, at this sacred feast, the glory of your holy name. **Amen**.

Jesus on the way to Emmaus

Luke 24: 13-27

bless you, and give thanks to you, O Lord Jesus Christ, the way, the truth, and the life, and our Saviour and our Redeemer, for your gracious appearance in the form of a stranger to the two disciples as they journeyed. How friendly was the manner in which you joined them on the road, as they were mourning over your Passion, and were conversing not about wars or the petty affairs of this life, but about your good deeds, your holy words, and your miracles. In spite of this, however, they could not but be very sad until the truth was made known to them, because they doubted your resurrection, and were not convinced about the vision of angels and what had been told them by their companions.

And who could better teach them, or better put an end to their doubts, than you, O Jesus, their good Master, the way, the truth, and the life, who manifested yourself to them, and gave them in the breaking of bread a token by which they knew you well? And so it came to pass; for shortly after you had joined them, and had gone a little way with them, you asked them (as if you had been an unknown stranger) what was the reason of the great sadness which oppressed them, saying: 'What are these discourses that you hold one with another as you walk, and are sad?'

I praise you, therefore, and magnify your holy name for the friendliness of your converse with those two disciples as they journeyed. Sad at heart and perplexed were they about your Passion and your condemnation to death: but you comforted them, and did perfectly instruct them by proofs and warrants of Holy Scripture,

86

in the Law and in the Prophets and in the Psalms. I praise you, and give thanks to you, O most gracious Lord Jesus, for your handling, expounding, and making clear and plain those passages of Scripture which before were obscure, involved with various metaphors, and understood by few. I bless you, O crown of the saints, most holy Lord Jesus Christ, Teacher of teachers, and Master of all laws and decrees, for opening in the days of old the mouths of the prophets, and now for vouchsafing to reveal the hidden things of the Scriptures to babes and to men who were unlearned, so that you might lead them to believe in you, in all your words, and in all your doings.

How joyous must have been their countenances as they heard you speaking to them; with what love must their cold hearts have been inflamed as you unfolded to them the meaning of the Word of God; for among lawgivers and interpreters of mysteries there was never one like you! How light you made each hour; how pleasant you made the whole day until eventide, when you went in with them, and they set food before you! How anxious were they that you should stop with them, desiring to listen to you all night, and to learn more and more from you!

And why? Because never upon earth did man discourse so excellently as did that stranger. No prophet, no king, no priest, no Levite, no son or disciple of the prophets, who worked miracles, or taught the hidden things of God; no saint; not even all the angelic choir, can compare with you, O stranger, as a teacher.

'We pray you, therefore, O Lord, to abide with us. It is towards evening, and the day is far spent; it is too late for you to go farther; speak yet awhile with us; gladly would we hear more from you; we are not tired or drowsy; we long to do as you bid us; for your words are sweeter than honey and the honeycomb; more precious are they than gold and silver, and nothing that man can wish for is to be compared with them.'

Would that I had been there, and could have walked unseen by Jesus' side, or could have followed behind, so as carefully to have noted all the words of my Lord Jesus Christ, to have lovingly treasured in my heart what I heard, so as to have been able to meditate often thereupon to my great profit!   **Amen**.

Jesus breaks bread

Luke 24: 28-35

I bless you, and give thanks to you, O Lord Jesus Christ, bread of life, sweet guest of the soul, and giver of heavenly grace, for your wondrous condescension in accepting as a friend the hospitality of the two disciples. With loving words and entreaties they asked you to enter the house; with their hands they constrained you; without you they would not enter the house or sit down to meat. Therefore, O loving and gentle Lord, moved by their earnest entreaties you went in to eat with them, and to speak to them delightful words about the food for souls prepared by the angels in our heavenly home.

Not as yet fully known to them, you sat at table with them, and as was your custom you took bread from the table into your sacred hands, and raising your right hand you blessed it with your sacred lips, even as you had previously blessed it before the eyes of your disciples when they sat at table with you. Then, after having first broken off a part which you ate yourself, you stretched forth your hand and offered it to them as to beloved friends; and at once their eyes were opened, and they recognized your divine power in the breaking of the hard bread, without the use of knife or other instrument, and in its exquisite flavour, when, renewing their gladness, you handed it to them as a token of friendship and of a wonder wrought for them. How joyous must have been that meal at which bread was eaten which had been blessed by the Lord's own hand! How blest were the eyes which recognized the Lord in the breaking of the bread which had been blessed by the mouth of God! But alas how brief was the duration of that happy moment, of that blessed meal! 'And he vanished out of their sight.'

'Where do you go, O Lord; why do you so soon leave those men?'

'Marvel not: take it not amiss: I know what I have done; I know what I am about to do. Other sheep I have to visit, to comfort, and to confirm in the faith. They wait for me, and long greatly to see me. To them therefore I go, in order that they may see me, and may rejoice, and may no more doubt my words. I must show to them my wounds, in order that when they have seen those evident signs they may firmly believe in me, may pay no further heed to the reasonings of men, and may no more deny my power. Nothing is impossible with me; the very elements obey my will.'

I praise and magnify you, most sweet Jesus, for all your doings, for all your blessed words, and for your appearances to your disciples scattered in various places. You would not leave as orphans those who were mourning and bewailing you. With a love which knew no bounds they ever longed to behold your face, to speak with you, to walk with you, to be in the ship with you, to lodge with you, to eat and drink with you, to be with you in vigil and in prayer, in sleeping and in uprising, and in promptly obeying every command that fell from your lips.

Earlier, when they were hot and tired by reason of a long journey you bade them to take a little rest, saying to them: 'Come apart into a desert place, where your eyes will not behold the vanities of the world, nor your ears be troubled by any distracting sounds, and rest for a while in meditation on the things of God, and in forgetfulness of those things which perish when used.'

Give me a clear understanding of difficult passages in Holy Scripture; and, where the meaning of your Word is plain and spiritual, kindle in my heart the fire of your love, as you did in the hearts of the two disciples, which were warmed by your appearance to them and by your discourse; so that, being refreshed on their journey by the Word of God as well as by the food of which they partook, they gave thanks and said: 'Was not our heart burning within us concerning Jesus, whilst He spoke in the way, and opened to us the Scriptures?' **Amen**.

Jesus appears in Jerusalem

John 20: 19-23

 bless you, and give thanks to you, O Lord Jesus Christ, peace of the godly, hope of the just, joy of faithful people gathered together in your name, comforter of the contrite in heart, and visitor of religious communities, for your glorious and miraculous appearance to your apostles assembled together, when it was already late. No one knocked and no one opened: the windows and doors of the house had been tightly closed as a precaution for fear of the Jews. And this no doubt happened in order that your entrance and appearance might be seen to be truly and certainly due to divine power alone, and not to any human power or agency, nor to any trick artfully contrived by the devil; for you are very God, who does not deceive.

But the simple and the devout, such as were the apostles and the other disciples assembled at that time in the upper room, you both visited and enlightened; and so you comforted and lovingly greeted them with the words, 'Peace be unto you; it is I, be not afraid.'

I praise and honour you for your gentle and peaceful greeting of them after their distress which had been so great, and I clap my hands at the thought of a sight which must have been more than ever joyous as following so great trouble and alarm. They did indeed need to be visited, to be comforted, supported, and greeted anew. They had been lying under tribulations and temptations greater than they had ever before passed through; they had all fled like sheep when the shepherd of the flock was seized and put to death; and after having been scattered hither and thither they were so fearful and sad that, even now when it was late, they had only just taken heart to meet together and breathe again, as it were, once more.

I praise and magnify your sweet name, which is . . . , O most loving Jesus, above all in heaven or on earth, for that you vouchsafed to show yourself on this day to the terrified fugitives, to your unhappy and saddened apostles, who had lost all heart, and no longer believed what you had so often told them about yourself. But now you unspeakably gladdened their hearts by friendly converse with them; you put an end to all their doubt and fear by at once openly showing to them in your hands and feet and sacred side evident signs of your Passion: in their sight you ate some broiled fish and some honey-comb; and in order that they might have the joy of eating with you handed to them with your own divine hand that which was left: during the meal you cited Holy Scripture, dissolved their doubts and made hidden things plain; you enlightened their understanding; you kindled their cold affections, and taught and explained to them what was needful and wholesome for them. Moreover, twice you gave your peace to them with your heavenly blessing, so that they rejoiced with exceeding great joy at having seen the Lord their God. And presently, so as to strengthen them against all unbelieving gainsayers, and to blot out their misdeeds, you breathed upon them the grace of the Holy Spirit, saying to them: 'Receive ye [given, as the greatest of all gifts, to you who for my name's sake have forsaken the world] – receive ye the Holy Ghost: whose sins you shall forgive, they are forgiven them; and whose sins you shall retain, they are retained.'

How great indeed was the grace given to the apostles by the breathing upon them of the Holy Spirit by the mouth of Christ rising from the dead by the glory of the Father, so that not only were they themselves made safe and absolved from all their sins, but also full power was given to them of absolving others from their sins, of repelling the unworthy, and of binding the guilty! How glorious was that day and how blessed was that evening hour when Jesus came to the apostles with such glory and such joy, filling them with heavenly gifts. **Amen**.

EASTER 6

Jesus and Thomas

John 20: 24-31

bless you, and give thanks to you, O Lord Jesus Christ, author of life, bestower of pardon, fountain of grace, promiser of glory to be enjoyed with the holy angels in everlasting bliss. I thank you, O Lord, for your gracious second appearance to all the apostles when Thomas, who till then had doubted, was present. This you brought about in order that you might confirm him in the true and perfect faith, by allowing him to see and handle your glorious body, adorned as it was with the sacred prints of your five wounds, memorials of your most holy Passion for the salvation of mankind.

I praise and glorify you for your joyful greeting, for showing yourself openly to your apostles, and for that heavenly benediction with which you blessed the apostles with your own sacred lips, saying to them with cheerful countenance: 'Peace be unto you, both now and in time to come: now indeed by faith and grace, but hereafter face to face, and by open vision: as the Father hath loved me, even so love I you: abide in my love, and continue with me; so will I abide with you, both now and for ever.'

I praise and glorify you, O Jesus Christ, adorable Master and Lord, for your friendly greeting of peace, and for your adorable condescension in standing in the midst of your disciples to keep them from fear of the Jews. For, as a good shepherd stands in the midst of his sheep to defend them from the fangs of wolves, so you dealt with your apostles in their evil day, protecting them for the kingdom of heaven's sake against those things which were against them. And as a mighty king and noble prince stands armour-clad in the midst of his people, grasping spear and shield to withstand the darts of the enemy, while he encourages his soldiers to fight bravely, and either conquer or die happily, even so, O most brave Jesus, you stood in the midst of your disciples, clad in a robe of gladness and with the breastplate of immortality, as a warrior against evil spirits and perverse men.

As proof of your identity you bore the marks of your Passion, gaping wounds in the shield of your body, with which you vanquished the princes of this world and the rulers of outer darkness; so that you might confirm in faith, hope, and charity your soldiers, the apostles, who on seeing your Passion, your death on the Cross, and your burial in the tightly-sealed tomb, had grievously lost heart. And who, indeed, having witnessed all those evident signs of death in you, could ever have thought that you would rise again to life?

It was in order that your beloved disciples, who were not yet fully confirmed in the faith, might not despair, that you showed yourself to them in visible form, with the wounds of your sacred and glorious body miraculously preserved, in proof of the reality of your resurrection; and it was in order that they might believe, and might no longer doubt of your actual appearance to them, that you said to them: 'Handle me, and see that I am that very Jesus Christ who for your sake hung upon the Cross, and by the power of God rose again the third day, as I so often plainly foretold you, though you did not then clearly understand me. Behold then now my hands and my feet, and my side, and above all mark well in me the five wounds of my Passion: meditate on them day and night, and think how great was the love I bore you, and how great were the sufferings I endured in order that you might have eternal life. Peace be to you, my friends, to you who despise the world, to you for whom, after you shall have overcome the many dangers of this present life, I have prepared everlasting joy in heaven with the holy angels. Fear not, be not of little faith: I am your reward, I am your crown, I am your abundant blessing!' **Amen**.

Thomas and the wounds

John 20: 24-29

Lord Jesus Christ, enlightener of faithful ones amidst the darkness of this world, I bless you, and give thanks to you, for the surpassing mercy shown to your holy apostle Thomas. By your special appearance to him, you strengthened him in believing in your resurrection – which passes all human understanding, and except by faith and divine revelation is incomprehensible to fallen man. Many are the marvellous works, O Lord God, that you have wrought since the foundation of the world; and even now you work marvels in heaven and on earth that they may declare the glory of your name. But although the mind of man cannot comprehend or fathom them, yet to you are they no hard task: they are wrought, and are ordained, chiefly for the salvation of the elect.

It was because your disciple, who was dear to you, did not persist in his opinion, and because he had no evil intent when he said he would not believe except he should see you and touch you – for this reason doubtless it was that he was found worthy to obtain so great mercy and grace as to be allowed to see you openly with his eyes, and reverently to touch you with his hand; and this so unmistakably that all his doubt was at an end, and he was able to confirm in the faith those who were faint-hearted. Being convinced then of your manhood, and believing from the heart that the Godhead was hidden therein, full of devotion and faith he exclaimed: *'My Lord, and my God.* This I firmly believe, this I honestly profess, this I openly declare, this I boldly proclaim, this I make known and long to tell forth to all the world, in order that all men may believe in you and be saved – *My Lord and my God*, my Creator and my Redeemer! This is the true and established faith which leads to the kingdom of heaven those who hold it.'

How great and how abounding is your sweetness, O Lord, which you have laid up for your saints, and for your chosen ones who are so dear to you; and how often, even in this life, do you show it to them in their times of trouble and distress, giving them as it were a foretaste of it, and encouraging them, both by word and by example, to press on and to persevere. Sometimes, indeed, you hide yourself, in order that by mourning they may be led to seek you and long to behold you, and that by falling and growing cold they may come to know their own weakness, and may cease to be presumptuous and to think more highly of themselves than they ought to think. And then once more you show yourself, comfort those who are sorrowful, enlighten them and teach them; so that in adversity they may not despair, nor in prosperity be puffed up, but may know themselves to be but men, mortal and sinful, needing the grace and mercy of God, and not angels already in glory.

I praise and extol your gracious tenderness in that, after granting peace and pardon to your holy apostle Thomas, as he knelt humbly and reverently before you, earnestly entreating your pardon, you manifested your love to him by showing to him your all-holy and glorious wound-prints, of more worth than all the treasures of the world, more precious than any jewels, more beauteous than the reddest of roses, sweeter than all spices or the sweetest-scented flowers. Those wounds are more beauteous than all the stars which bespangle the firmament of heaven; more than all else besides, those wounds rejoice the souls of the saints, inflame the hearts of sinners, and draw from them bitter tears; they rouse the slothful to more earnest prayers; they lead the devout to kiss them over and over again; they move men of good-will to fervent thankfulness.

The frequent remembrance and earnest contemplation of those wounds of Christ so stirred the inmost soul of the holy and most devout Francis of Assisi and made his eyes so run with tears, that their all-holy prints could be plainly seen upon his own body. And to this day those five holy wounds of Jesus, worthy of all love, stir to their inmost depths the hearts of many devout Christians; the sight of those wounds brings tears to their eyes, as they gaze in church upon a picture of the Crucified, or hear the Passion of Christ preached, or read, or ponder thereon to the praise of God.   **Amen**.

A prayer for peace of heart

John 20: 19, 26

Lord Jesus Christ, fountain of sweetness, King of heaven and earth, true peace of hearts, and comforter of those who mourn, say, I beseech you, to my soul, which is troubled and distressed as you best know: 'I am your salvation, peace, life, comfort, hope, light and rest. In me is all your good, your soul's true comfort, the only happiness that is real and that knows no end. What more would you have?'

'Nothing, Lord; you alone would I have; you do I seek; you do I long for; you do I love from the bottom of my heart; you in everything, and above everything, everywhere and at all times, do I bless and praise. You rule over all things that are in heaven and on earth, in the sea and in all deep places, in the mountains and in the woods: to you is known every creature whether small or great; from your eye nothing is hid. In wisdom have you made all things, and by your providence are all things governed and preserved.'

Oh when will you come to me – peace of God that comes from that clear knowledge of my Maker which passes all reason and the understanding both of angels and of men? Oh when will you so fill me, both within and without, that nothing shall be left for me to desire? O Lord God, my heart can find no rest, until it rests in you! My mind can have no peace until it is perfectly united to you in that life which knows no end. O peace, how sweet, how precious is your name in all the world! How full of joy and gladness is your voice in our home which is above! O true, O supreme, O everlasting peace with God, with angels, and with men of good will!

Give me, O Lord, I pray you, peace in my heart, that I may love you above all things; give me peace in my mouth, that I may praise you with true devotion; give me peace in my hand that I may do all my good works for your honour! When I am sad, say to me: 'Peace be unto thee; it is I, be not afraid.' 'Peace be unto thee' – what can be more pleasant to me than this? 'It is I' – what possession can be more joyful than this? 'Be not afraid' – what cause of rejoicing can be more secure than this? 'Behold, I am with you' – what enjoyment can be more sweet from everlasting to everlasting than this, what surer and firmer ground can there be for believing, and for laying hold on life eternal?

Whatever, O Lord, I possess, whatever I see, whatever I long for, all is nothing without you. In you alone is all my wealth; there can be nothing better, nothing more perfect, nothing richer, nothing more blessed than you. In you, therefore, O God, my Saviour, is to be found all that I have and all that I hope for; all my safety, all my peace: nowhere else, in no created good, however lovely, however noble, however great, can I find it. I say, therefore, and I pray with holy and humble Francis of Assisi: 'My God, and my All! More I wish not for.' And if ever I should be in distress, and be deprived of inward consolation and comfort, still would I say and pray: 'My God, and my All!' I want nothing, I wish for nothing, O my God, but for you, who are all in all, who are above all and before all are blessed for ever. Give me grace, O Lord, to meditate intently upon these things, and ever faithfully to fulfil them. **Amen.**

EASTER 9

Jesus appears on Mount Tabor

Matt. 28: 19-20

 bless you, and give thanks to you, O Lord Jesus Christ, King of heaven and earth, who weighs the mountains in a balance, and holds the earth in the hollow of your hand, who sits above the cherubim and the seraphim, looking down upon the depths beneath, who walks above the stars of heaven, who observes the ends of the earth, who knows all things before they have their being.

I praise and glorify you, O Jesus, for your great goodness in having summoned your disciples to this holy and private place, shut off from the noise of the world, a place fit to be chosen for the delivery of your divine commands. On that spot you had already been transfigured – the other apostles being absent – in the presence of three chosen witnesses, Peter, James and John; and as a voice from the Father came from heaven, you were clothed and adorned with an excellent brightness; and by a revelation, of which they alone were witnesses, your majesty was, before your Passion, made known to your disciples for the confirmation of their faith.

In this more public appearance, however, after your most glorious resurrection, you manifested yourself to a larger number of your disciples, in order thereby to confirm the faith of those who believed; to convince the doubting ones; lovingly to instruct and rejoice the hearts of all by your presence, and by manifesting to them the power over everything in heaven and on earth given you by the Father. When, therefore, with your own lips you declared these things to them, those who were then present with you adored you and glorified your holy Name. Prostrating themselves at your feet, they rejoiced in singing with the deepest devotion a new hymn to you, our God; for mysteries concerning the Holy Trinity so deep and wondrous were then made known to them, that no one can fully give expression to them. How glorious and entrancing was that vision; how unfathomable and divine that revelation; how great and unspeakable was the joy that filled the hearts of the holy apostles!

I praise and glorify you, O most sweet and most gentle Jesus, for having conversed so graciously with your disciples on the Mount; for your revelation to them of the true faith of the Holy Trinity; and for your delivery to them of the right form of words for the baptism of the faithful, in water, for the remission of sins, 'in the Name of the Father, and of the Son and of the Holy Ghost.' Amen. In these words, as I believe, was I myself baptized by a faithful priest; and thereafter I was in the bosom of holy Church, by faithful parents, educated and instructed in the right and catholic faith.

For this I give thanks to you, O Christ; for it is from you that every good gift comes, and the hope of life eternal – to which hope, O Lord, vouchsafe to bring me when the hour of my departure shall come. It is for me to pray; it is for you to help. I am weak and unstable, you are full of loving-kindness and mercy; you can deliver me from distress of every kind; you can bring me to the mount of Glory. O Jesus, saving health of my countenance, and my God, to you do I cry; for you do I long; to you do I pray by day and by night, till, by the help of your grace alone, I shall be brought in safety to you, who with the Father and the Holy Spirit live and reign; one God, world without end. **Amen**.

A prayer of thanksgiving

John 17: 4-5

 most sweet Lord Jesus Christ, who desires my everlasting salvation, I, a man poor and weak, and undeserving of any comfort or any good thing, would bless you; and, together with your saints and elect, would glorify for ever your most holy name.

Chiefly do I thank you for having, of your great love and pity, willed to become man for me, to take my nature upon you, outside the course of nature to be conceived by the Holy Spirit, and to be miraculously born of Mary, a pure virgin; to be suckled and nourished; to be circumcised; and to be presented in the Temple, in order that you might cleanse me from every impurity of mind and body, and might teach me to live soberly, righteously and chastely all my days.

Still more, and every day and hour of my life, do I thank you for your most holy and most bitter Passion; for it was for me that you vouchsafed to suffer, to be crucified, to die and to be buried, in order that by your sinless death you might deliver me from everlasting death, and might by your example strengthen me to be patient under adversity.

Further, with a heart full of joy, do I thank you for having, for my consolation, risen on the third day from the tomb, and given great joy to your disciples by appearing to them in the upper room when the doors were shut; doing this that I may not despair in any tribulation of my own, or when any harm or danger befalls me, but may trust in you for deliverance from my present trouble, and may have a sure hope of being at the last day raised by you, together with your elect, to everlasting life.

Yet, again, do I most devoutly thank you, rejoicing with them, not only with my lips, but from the bottom of my heart, for that august procession to Bethany, and for your glorious Ascension into heaven, in the presence of your holy mother and other disciples. You went before to prepare for me a place with you; and to open to me by your Passion and your Cross the gate of the kingdom of heaven, where with the angels you now live and reign in the everlasting glory of the Father, until such time as you shall return at the end of the world to judge both the living and the dead. This it was which was taught us by the two holy angels clothed in white garments (a symbol of joy) who at that time appeared to your disciples, as they were looking up after you to heaven. Oh how blessed were the eyes which were found worthy to behold you in the flesh; and how blessed were the ears which heard you speaking of the kingdom of God, than which nothing can be found more delightful to hear about, nothing more blessed to enjoy!

It was for me that you did ascend into the highest heavens, above the angels in their serried ranks, to that place where dwell those blessed ones who even now reign with you in your excellent glory. You ascended, in order that all my hope might be set on things above, and might be lifted up to you, instead of being fixed on things earthly, and seeking its delight in them. Apart from God there is nothing which is not empty and transient, worthless and of no account. Everything which keeps me back from God, and stands in the way of devout prayer and meditation upon heavenly things, is to be spurned and put aside.

I beseech you, therefore, O most loving Jesus, King of everlasting glory, that in the kingdom of your Father you would remember me, the least of all your servants, and would send to me now from heaven the Holy Spirit, the Paraclete, to be my true Comforter, and to give me renewed zeal and a larger outpouring of spiritual gifts. **Amen**.

The angels in white

Acts 1: 1-11

 bless and praise you, O most sweet Jesus Christ, and on this holy day devoutly do I thank you for having (after your departure from the apostles and your entrance with the angels into heaven) sent two angels clad in white, messengers of the court of heaven, to comfort your bereaved ones who were looking up after you into heaven, but were unable to follow you. *'Ye men of Galilee,'* they said to them, *'Ye men of Galilee, why stand you looking up to Heaven?* Why marvel you at this astounding miracle, the like of which was never seen? With God all things are possible; God, made Man, has gone up with a shout, even as in the psalm it was foretold of him. Be it your task, therefore, to carry the tidings, and to bear witness, with and to others, of the things which you have heard and seen, even as it was commanded you. *This Jesus who is taken up from you into Heaven, shall so come as you have seen him going into Heaven.* But he who till now, in order that he might lead to the realms above those who humbly followed him upon earth, here showed himself to you as One meek and lowly, will then come in great power and glory to judge the living and the dead.'

O my Jesus, whom I love above all things, remember, I beseech you, in your glory, me, poor sinner that I am. Remember and have mercy on me, left a stranger and an exile in this vale of tears, mourning and weeping amid the many temptations and troubles of this present life, which so often keep back my heart from thinking of the joys of heaven. Draw me, then, after you, O most blessed Jesus, so that, unable as I am to follow you with my bodily feet, I may at least go after you in spirit, by the path of holy desire and burning love. All unworthy, all unable, as I am, to behold you in the unfathomableness of your divine majesty, give me grace to follow the example of humility which in your human nature you set me.

O blessed sight, to behold God face to face, as he is in himself, as he is even now perfectly seen in heaven by the angels and all the saints. And now I know of a truth that never can all my desires be satisfied or set at rest by any earthly good. That can only be when I am united to you, my God, in heaven, and am purged from all that is evil. But for this it was that you went before me to the Father, to prepare the way and a place where I may dwell with you; and to obtain for me, by the scars of your wounds, the pardon of my sins, so that I may have great confidence before you, both in this life and in that which is to come, by reason of the abundance of your mercies, the all-sufficiency of your merits, and the assistance of the prayers of all the saints and angels.

Ah, good Jesus, forsake me not! You who in the power of your might have wrought great marvels, you are my love, and that which my soul longs for; you are my Saviour and Redeemer, my hope from my youth up, my expectation, and that in which I place all my trust even unto old age. Thanking you from the bottom of my heart for all your benefits, I will, with all your saints, love you and praise you above all things, all the days of my pilgrimage and of my exile here on earth.

And now, O my soul, go back with Mary, the mother of Jesus, and with his apostles, from the Mount of Olives to the City of Jerusalem, there to seek peace of heart and rest from all the cares of the world. Go up with them to that large upper room, where the Passover of the old Law was superseded by the institution of the adorable sacrament of the body of Christ, there ordained and given to the apostles. Recollect yourself therefore; remain quietly alone and in silence; wait upon God in prayers and devout meditation, and so prepare yourself against the approaching feast of Pentecost, for receiving, as did the apostles, with a fervent heart the Holy Spirit of God. They took no thought of earthly comfort, but awaited, in the privacy of that upper room, the new pledge of love to be sent by Christ from heaven. Call to mind meanwhile the good gifts of God from the beginning of the world until now, and chiefly occupy yourself in conferring with the blessed Virgin Mary about the Incarnation of Christ; and think over all the sayings and doings of Jesus her Son, as recorded in the Gospels, from the day of his birth to the day of his glorious Ascension to the Father. **Amen**.

The sending of the Holy Spirit

Acts 2

 bless you, and give thanks to you, O Lord Jesus Christ, kind comforter of the sorrowful, most sweet visitor of the sick, most powerful helper of those in trouble, for your true and faithful promise of divine gifts to be sent down from your home in heaven, and from the Father of lights. I thank you for your inestimable bounty, and for the wondrous outpouring of the multiform grace of the Holy Spirit upon your disciples gathered together in Jerusalem. They were assembled in the upper room, praying and waiting anxiously for the consolation of the Holy Spirit from heaven: they were not thinking about the things of this life; but, like devout monks dwelling apart from the tumult of the world, in quietude and silence, they had cast all earthly cares out of their minds, and with their hearts fixed upon those joys which last for ever, they were preparing themselves by fervent prayer for receiving yet fuller gifts of grace.

I praise and glorify you, O most glorious Jesus Christ, king of the holy angels, for the right joyous festival of this day, and for the benediction and hallowing year by year by the priest (in the power of the Holy Spirit) of the sacred font, in which those who are baptized in the name of the Holy Trinity are cleansed from all their sins, become partakers of everlasting life, and by the grace of the Holy Spirit are made meet to be accounted heirs of the kingdom of heaven, and fellow-citizens of the angels.

I praise and glorify you for having adorned this most holy day with many miracles and signs and gifts, and for having commanded it to be for ever observed by the faithful with joyous devotion. It was on this day that in old time the Law was given by Moses upon

Mount Sinai to your people Israel, when they had been delivered from the heavy yoke of bondage, and had come forth from the land of Egypt to sacrifice to you in the wilderness, where you gave them for food sweet manna from heaven. And it was for the perpetual remembrance of this deliverance that you commanded a special sacrifice of thanksgiving to be year by year offered to you of the newly gathered fruits of the harvest.

But now, under the new covenant, after you had with great power ascended into heaven far above all angels, with yet fuller grace and bounty you distinguished, blessed, and consecrated this holy day; and in place of sweet manna you sent, by a visible sign from heaven, the Holy Spirit upon your apostles – with a loud noise, fiery tongues appearing upon each of them – in order that inwardly they might be inflamed with love, and outwardly might be ready and eloquent of speech, so as boldly to proclaim, as the Holy Spirit inspired them and gave them utterance, all the mighty works which in the land of the Jews you had wrought for our salvation. Very many indeed were they, and such as to men were impossible; but to God all things are possible and easy. Then was fulfilled that which was spoken by the prophet Isaiah, saying: 'The law shall come forth from Sion, and the word of the Lord from Jerusalem.' Never before had such marvels been heard of as those of this day, when all at once so many faithful men and women received the Holy Spirit by a visible sign, that is, by tongues of fire; prophesied so that all could understand; interpreted Holy Scripture, and spoke the languages of all nations; when men unversed in books or letters were, in the school of God, at once and perfectly instructed by the Holy Spirit, and besides receiving so much knowledge, were also made illustrious by working many miracles and prodigies.

How wondrous and beyond description is the power of the Holy Spirit! He makes all whom he visits, and into whom he enters, zealous and learned, humble and devout, joyous and strong. Learning comes at once where the Holy Spirit is the inward Teacher, revealing the secret things of God even to babes, as seems to him expedient for their salvation and for the good of others. Especially does he teach his own disciples and secret friends to despise the world, not to set their minds on high things, but ever to condescend to things that are lowly; to think meanly of themselves; to avoid distractions; and to take account of their faults and to bewail them. May he work in me for Jesus' sake! **Amen**.

Fourteen Meditations

for

Christmas

The promise of a Messiah

John 1: 19-28

 almighty and most gracious God, whose nature is goodness, whose will is power, whose property it is to have mercy, I bless you, and give thanks to you for your infinite love, and for your free and undeserved goodness. You lost no time in calling back man, who had been taken captive in the snare of the devil, and brought low by the poison of a mortal disease, from both his manifold wanderings from the right way, and from the defilement of his sins, into the way of repentance, and a state of righteousness; by giving to him, through the saving promise of your coming, the hope of pardon, and the prospect of a remedy to be brought within his reach.

And lest man should at any time seek to plead ignorance as an excuse for the malice of his sin, you gave him frequent warning of the error of his ways, by revealing to him the Law, by smiting him with a heavy hand, by exercising open judgements upon sinners, by working frequent miracles, and by promising good things to come; so that they might be without excuse who should not turn to you as their God, and to a knowledge of the truth.

For all through the five ages of the world, by means of patriarchs, of judges, of priests, of kings, and of prophets, from righteous Abel even unto John the Baptist, your forerunner, you never ceased, by wonderful miracles and manifold prophecies, to foretell, to promise, and to prefigure your coming, without which we are undone: so that by means of so many witnesses going before you, and proclaiming your mysteries, you might implant in our minds the grace of faith, and by the lively examples of so many ancient fathers, might kindle in our dull cold hearts the fire of your love.

Glory be to the Father, and to the Son and to the Holy Ghost, as it was in the beginning, is now and shall be forever. **Amen**.

Redemption by the Incarnate Word

Luke 1: 26-56; 2: 1-7; John 1:14

bless you, and give thanks to you, my Lord and my God, Creator and Redeemer of the human race, for your exceeding great love in willing that man, whom you had wonderfully created, should be still more wonderfully redeemed. For it was when we were yet your enemies, and death had long tyrannized over all the human race, that you called to mind your rich mercies, and from the place of your habitation in glory, you looked down upon this vale of tears and wretchedness.

It was when you saw that the affliction of your people was great upon the earth, and that the burden of the sons of Adam was grievous to be borne, that, inwardly moved by the tenderness of your charity, you set yourself to think, on our behalf, thoughts of redemption and of peace.

For, when the fullness of time was come, you, yourself, the Dayspring from on high, came to visit us, and fulfilled the desires of the prophets by taking our flesh, and appearing among men as true God and true man.

I bless and praise you, Jesus Christ, our Saviour, for your exceeding great humility in deigning to choose for your mother a poor young maiden, and for causing her to be espoused to the poor carpenter Joseph, a just and holy man.

I bless you for making known your most illustrious Incarnation, and for the reverent angelic greeting, with which the angel Gabriel most devoutly saluted the ever-blessed virgin Mary, making known to her the divine mystery that she should be the mother of the Son of God.

I praise and magnify you for the grandeur of the faith of Mary the virgin, for the courage of her assent, for the lowliness of her reply, and for all the other virtues which she so conspicuously displayed, when she made her obedient answer to the angel's message in the words: 'Behold the handmaid of the Lord, be it done to me according to Thy word.'

I praise and glorify you, O eternal Wisdom of the Father, for your marvellous condescension in entering the prison of our mortal frame, and for your most pure conception, by the operation of the Holy Spirit upon Mary; in whose virgin womb the Power of the most Highest, overshadowing her, formed your most sacred body from the undefiled flesh of a pure virgin. For, being at the same time true God, consubstantial with the eternal Father, you were made one flesh with us, without spot of sin, to make us one spirit with you, through the adoption of the sons of God.

I praise and magnify you for voluntarily emptying yourself of divine fullness,and for graciously taking upon yourself our weak and degraded nature, capable of suffering and of death; so that you might fill us by emptying yourself, might save us by your sufferings, might raise us by your lowliness, might strengthen us by your weakness, and by your death might bring us to a glorious immortality.

I praise and magnify you, because you (whose divine nature knows neither times nor seasons, but who has ordered all things here below in their season and time), vouchsafed to dwell for nine long months within the narrow limits of a virgin's womb, and to lie hid there as a babe waiting for the due time of his birth.

O the gracious and most wondrous condescension of him, who, though God of boundless glory, did not think it scornful to become a mere creature; and who, though he had created all things by his own will, yet, to free us from them, was ready to take upon himself our sorrows!

O most sweet Jesus, the brightness of the eternal Glory, the lower you made yourself by taking our nature, the more exalted do you appear to me in your goodness; and the more you identify with sinners, the dearer you become to me. Glory be to you, O Lord Jesus Christ.   **Amen**.

CHRISTMAS 3

Jesus is born in poverty

Luke 2: 6-7

 bless, and give thanks to you, O Lord Jesus Christ, the only-begotten of the Father, born before all worlds, who, of your unspeakable condescension, did vouchsafe to be born in a filthy stable, and for the love of holy poverty, to be laid in a narrow manger.

I praise you, most loving Jesus, for your illustrious origin; for your glorious birth of the pure virgin Mary; for your poverty; and for your humility in lying in so poor and mean a crib. Who can meditate as he should on the thought of the most High God, so demeaning himself for our sake? O what thanks the human race owes to you, who, for its redemption, chose to lie in a narrow manger!

O boundless tenderness, O wondrous sweetness, O sweetest love – God born a helpless babe, wrapped in mean swaddling clothes, laid in a narrow manger, with brute beasts surrounding him!

O humility passing human thought, that the Lord of all lords should deign to become the fellow-servant of his own servants! But, O my Lord, and my God, it seemed to you too small a thing, that you, my Creator, should also be my Father; you even stooped to become my Brother, and to be made flesh of my flesh, taking in very truth my nature (sin only excepted).

O Birth, outside the course of nature, triumphing over the natural order of our births, and assuaging by divine power the tears which we shed at them, in order that, by it, our nature might be restored!

O how blessed and how lovely was your nativity, O sweetest Jesus, child of the illustrious virgin; by your birth from the womb of your highly exalted mother Mary, you make good the faults of our birth, renew our condition, cancel our condemnation and blot out the handwriting of the decree which was against us; so that, if a man is tempted to repine at being born of Adam's stock, he may rejoice in your undefiled nativity, and in the most blessed trust that by your grace he has been born again.

I thank you, for your self-chosen and glorious nativity, O Lord Jesus Christ, the only-begotten Son of God, by whom we have access to that grace in which we stand, and trust in the hope restored to us from above of the glory of the sons of God. You are the pledge of our redemption: you are the everlasting hope of all men; to you do we sinners humbly fly for refuge – to you, who came to seek us, when as yet we knew you not.

O sweet and holy infancy, from which alone true innocency comes to human hearts; by which, however old a man may be, he may go back to blessed infancy, and may be made like to you, not by the shrinking of his limbs, but by the lowliness of his mind, and the holiness of his life!

O most gentle Jesus, who, in order to give to all men an example of a holy life, and the means of everlasting salvation, willed to be born of Mary the virgin, at the hour of midnight, grant that I may tread in the sacred footsteps of your humility and poverty! Grant that I may join (in giving praise and thanks to you) the angels and the whole company of the heavenly host, whom you caused to be the joyful heralds of your nativity!   **Amen**.

CHRISTMAS 4

(a) Jesus, a fragile baby

Luke 2: 6-7

 bless you, and give thanks to you, O Lord Jesus Christ, for that, as soon as you had taken your flesh, you endured for love of us many hardships, and faced the bitterness of the stress of utter poverty. For when you, as very God, were born into the world, you chose for the hour of your birth the secrecy of the night, and for its ease and comfort the winter cold: you did not seek, as a home for your sovereign Majesty, the grandeur of a stately palace, but found instead, in a little crib, a shelter for your infant helplessness.

O poverty beyond compare, that you could scarce find swaddling clothes with which to wrap yourself – you who hold the world in the hollow of your hand, who in wondrous variety adorn the sky with stars, the earth with flowers, and beasts with their coats of hair.

O holy poverty of the Son of God, more precious than all earthly wealth, poverty in which scarce one of us can follow you! For which of us has come into the world in straits such as yours?

To you, then, O my Jesus, mighty King, Infant worthy of all love; to you do I offer from the bottom of my heart the tribute of all the gratitude of which my heart is capable, beseeching you that you would grant me lovingly to cherish the joys of holy poverty, and by the help of your grace to bear its hardships patiently. You left your throne on high that you might commend the state of poverty to our love. To your riches, as God, no limits can be set: but as man, for our sakes, you made yourself poor.

I praise and magnify you, for taking upon yourself our poverty and weakness; and for holding us so dear, that laying aside your royal diadem, you vouchsafed to be numbered among the sons of men, and as if you had been one of them, to share the frailty of our nature, yet without any spot of sin. **Amen**.

114

(b) Jesus, a weeping infant

Luke 2: 6-7

I bless you, and give thanks to you, O Lord Jesus Christ, joy of angels, comforter of the sad at heart, for your infant crying and tears, with which you sorrowfully mourned over the sins of the sons of Adam.

O thing of wonder, O surpassing condescension, that he who is very God should cry in a cradle as a helpless babe; that he, to whom in heaven angels sing praise, should, as one subject to death, hang upon a mother's breasts; that he who sustains and gives food to all flesh, who makes the clouds to thunder, and the rain to water the earth, should be held by the hand, and be carried about as a helpless child!

How is that which is highest joined with that which is lowest, that which is of man with that which is of God!

It was to wash me from my iniquity that, as an infant, you wept; it was over my sins that your tears were shed. Therefore, O my Lord and my God, I owe you more for the sorrows, by which you did redeem me, than for that mighty working by which you did create me. How ought I not to bewail my sins, since you, O Lord, wept so constantly over them! How grievous must have been the wounds of my soul, when the tears which you shed over them were so many!

And yet there is nothing strange or wondrous in the thought that you, who came down from heaven to shed your precious blood to wash us from our sins, should shed tears of pity for them.

I praise you, therefore, my beloved Jesus, and I will never cease to praise you, for the love and for the pity you have shown to me, a miserable, unworthy sinner. **Amen.**

Jesus at his mother's breasts

Luke 2: 6-7

I bless you, and give thanks to you, O Lord Jesus Christ, never-failing fountain of life, for being suckled at the breasts of Mary the virgin, by whose sacred milk you were fed – you who give food to all, you who are the food and bread of angels.

O the unspeakable sweetness of the condescension of God to man! Who can rightly think of the excellence of the mystery and the bounty of the undeserved mercy, that God should be suckled at a mother's breasts, and be nourished by a virgin's milk? O my Lord and my God, with what tenderness of love have you made yourself one with me, by thus subjecting yourself to the needs of our human weakness! O great and tremendous mystery that you, one and the same person, are made known to us as God of the substance of God and the Father, and very man of the substance of your virgin mother: that we confess you to be, at one and the same time, the son of a woman, and the only-begotten of the Father's glory: that you are made a partaker of our human nature, and yet, being one and the same person, are worshipped as the Lord of angels.

I praise you, therefore, and bless your infinitely tender love, because you did not think it scornful to be nourished at your mother's breasts, if so you might make it plain that you had indeed taken our flesh, of the substance of your virgin mother.

O you, who give food to all, and who were content with so little, feed my soul, I beseech you with the rich banquet of your holy Word, and give me grace to serve you and to give thanks to you so long as I shall dwell in this body, a frail tenement of clay. **Amen**.

Jesus is circumcised

Luke 2:21

Lord Jesus Christ, Saviour of the world, fountain of purity, pattern of spotless innocence, I bless you, and give thanks to you for the painful circumcision of your most tender flesh, according to the law of Moses; to which, in order that in all things you might conform to it, you submitted yourself, although you were without any spot of sin.

I praise you for the first spilling of your innocent blood, which on this day was shed for us. O most meek Lamb of God, how brightly were the excellence of your love and the depth of your patience shown forth, when, at so tender an age, you submitted your holy and innocent flesh to the pain of circumcision, a pain which it had not deserved.

It is I who have sinned; it is you who pay the penalty of my sin. I, indeed, was conceived and born in sin: you were conceived without sin, and yet you meekly submitted to be branded with a sinner's mark. What was there in you which was faulty, or useless, that needed to be cut away?

O most good and gracious Lord Jesus, you who did meekly undergo the circumcision of your innocent flesh, circumcise, I pray you, all my members with the cutting-stone of your grace; order all my actions, and direct all my ways, in conformity with your most holy life. All that you find in me unspiritual cut away and destroy: root out all that you see in me to be useless: keep down with all the needful force of your discipline whatever in me is false and frivolous; so that, inwardly cleansed from my faults, and adorned with the virtues that I lack, I may have a perpetual love of your holy name, and be found meet to dwell with you in the heavenly kingdom. **Amen.**

CHRISTMAS 7

The naming of Jesus

Matt. 1:21; Luke 2:21

I bless you, and give thanks to you, O Lord Jesus Christ, for the giving to you of your saving and adorable name, Jesus.

This name was first made known by the angel to blessed Mary the virgin; later it was revealed to holy Joseph in a dream; but now, on this day, it was given you by your parents.

O sweetest name of Jesus, name blessed above every name, whether in heaven or on earth! According to your name, O my Jesus, so be your praise to the ends of the world. From the rising of the sun to the going down thereof, may your glorious name be worthily magnified from this time forth for evermore! From everlasting was this most holy and adorable name made yours by God the Father; but only when the fullness of time was come, was it made known unto men. For there is no other name given to men, whereby we must be saved.

Just, therefore, and right is it, that to you should bow every knee in heaven and on earth; and that every tongue should confess that you are Jesus Christ, our Saviour and our Redeemer. O most sweet Jesus, how excellent is your name in all the earth! Great indeed is your name above the name of Solomon, and above those of all the kings which were before or after him. Therefore, all the kings of the earth shall fall down and worship you; and all peoples and languages shall serve and obey you; for you are the Lord our God, the King, and the Saviour of all Christians.

O sweet and saving name of Jesus, which heals all our infirmities, enlightens our minds, sets on fire our hearts, drives away our grief, softens anger, sheds forth peace and concord, fosters charity, and turns our sorrow into joy!

This dearest of all names was brought down to earth by an angel from heaven. This name was preached throughout the world by the apostles. For this name it was that the martyrs suffered. This name it was that confessors proclaimed aloud. This name it was that holy virgins ardently loved. This name it is which is praised and hymned by old and young. The most sweet name of Jesus it is which, rather than deny, thousands upon thousands of the faithful have preferred to suffer death.

This saving name it is which princes and kings now worship and adore. This name it is which priests and doctors publish and proclaim. This name it is which all faithful Christians especially venerate and love; for, renouncing the devil and the world, it is in the name of Jesus that they hope to be saved. For Jesus is the Saviour, and the Protector, of all who are his, and who believe in, and who love, him to the end.

O most sweet Jesus, my one hope of salvation, write, I beseech you, your name upon my heart, not in the letter but in the spirit; and grant that by your grace it may be so strongly there impressed, and may there remain, that neither prosperity nor adversity may ever dim my love for you. Be to me a strong tower from the face of the enemy, my comforter in tribulation, my counsellor when I am in doubt, my refuge in distress, my lifter-up when I fall, the model of my life, my restorer when I go astray, and my ever-faithful guide through all the dangers and temptations of this mortal life to my home which is above. **Amen**.

CHRISTMAS 8

The Epiphany

Matt. 2: 1-12

 bless you, and give thanks to you, O Lord Jesus Christ, Prince of the kings of the earth, for your glorious manifestation to the three kings. For after you had been born in Bethlehem of Judaea, you were not slow in revealing your majesty to men who came from afar; and having led them by a heavenly light to your humble resting-place, you manifested to them your holy poverty.

I praise your gracious mercy for these firstfruits of the Gentile world, and for your call to these strangers, whom, by a secret inspiration of your grace, you did draw from Eastern lands to behold the light of faith. Among the princes of Israel were found none who made ready, with such reverence and trust, to seek the place of your nativity: far more lively was the faith, far more fervent the devotion, of those strangers to the Mosaic covenant.

I glorify your holy name for your wondrous enlightenment of Gentiles; for so gloriously did you send forth your light into the hearts of those men of the East, who as yet were sitting in darkness, that without thinking of the length of their journey, they followed (with a trust which knew no doubt) the leading of the sign from heaven.

I reverently join the holy magi in adoring you; and, following them step by step, I would devoutly offer to you their three precious gifts, each containing a deep mystery. For, falling at your feet, they offered to you gold in token of your kingly dignity, frankincense as doing homage to your divine majesty, myrrh as confessing your submission to the law of death.

Wherefore, O my Lord Jesus Christ, most gracious King of kings, Ruler of heaven and of earth, accept, I beseech you, at the hand of your servant, the mystic offering, which I now humbly present to you.

I offer to you in the first place right faith, firm hope, and pure charity, in which I trust that I may continue to the end. I believe that you are the King of heaven and of earth: I adore you as very God, the only-begotten of the Father: I confess that, for my salvation, you took of the virgin Mary a mortal body.

Accept further, I beseech you, also these other gifts, each having in itself a sweet-smelling savour. I give to you that which also I received from you, namely all my worldly goods, which I renounce for love of you. I would not in this life have anything of my own. I wish to be content with common food and simple raiment. This is in a moral sense my oblation of pure gold.

I would add also the gift of frankincense, by which I mean the incense of devout prayer; beseeching you, with sighs and tears, for the forgiveness of my sins; praising and thanking you for the good gifts you have bestowed upon me; and grieving for all who are in trouble or distress. This, surely, is the burning of fragrant incense, acceptable to you.

I offer to you, also, in figure, myrrh, in memory of your most bitter Passion, praying that I too may have grace to run in the way of perfection by the austerity of my self-mortification. For, as often as (out of love of you) I call to mind the bitterness of your Passion, I offer to you, in figure, the choicest myrrh: and whenever I overcome in myself evil desires, and renounce my own will, I bruise, as best I may, in the mortar of my heart, fragrant myrrh, so that from this may come forth a sacrifice acceptable to you. Oh, how happy should I be, if I could offer to my Jesus a bundle of myrrh, by gathering together into one all the labour, all the sorrow, and all the bitterness of your Passion! For it is by such a mingling of myrrh and frankincense that the faithful soul is moved to earnest efforts after amendment, to acts of penance, and to the mortification of corrupt desires. Thanks be to God. **Amen**.

CHRISTMAS 9

(a) Jesus is taken into Egypt

Matt. 2: 13-23

 bless you, and give thanks to you, O Lord Jesus Christ, most mighty King of kings, for your persecution, and for the hardships forced upon you, in the days of your childhood. You fled from the face of the most wicked king Herod, driven forth as a stranger and an outcast from your own land, and had to enter in secret that land of Egypt, from which, in the days of old, you had led forth the children of Israel with a mighty hand.

I praise and magnify you for the toilsome journey and long exile, which you underwent, dwelling in a foreign land for the space of seven years, amidst a barbarous people, and men altogether strange to you.

How cruel was the wickedness which could seek to slay the Author of life, and could drive out, from the land into which he had been born, the King of heaven! What tears would not one have shed, could one have seen the graceful virgin mother, with her Child, so fair and so beloved, hurrying away, sheltered by the darkness of the night, to take refuge in a land of which they knew nothing! Truly this instance of persecution is to us a bright example of patience, and is a lesson to all Christ's people not to wonder at having to suffer many things at the hands of men who know him not.

I praise and magnify you, O Lord Jesus Christ, for your blessed return from Egypt; for journeying back again into your own land; for dwelling with your parents in Nazareth, as their son; for the innocent life led by you there among their friends and neighbours; and for submitting to share the poverty of your mother, and of her spouse, the holy Joseph.

122

Grant to me now, I beseech you, O my beloved Jesus, to tread, at least in my small degree, in your steps, in this matter of patience; give me grace not to murmur when I have to suffer wrong; but rather humbly to give way to an angry man, to submit cheerfully to being laughed at, and evil spoken of; and when any one vexes and annoys me, give me grace to curb my anger against him, to pray earnestly for his salvation, and so far as may be, to set down his fault to the account of the old serpent who led him into it.

Give me grace to live peaceably with my brethren, willing to give way to them, and with them patiently to bear, for your honour and glory, the lack of this world's goods, no matter how great it may be. **Amen**.

(b) The holy innocents

Matt. 2: 16-18

 bless you, and give thanks to you, O Lord Jesus Christ, hope of those who die young, glory of the lowly, and crown of all the saints, for the deaths of so many innocent children put to death on account of your holy name.

I praise and magnify you for these first fruits of the holy martyrs, who suffered without having ever sinned, whom you delivered out of this world pure in body and in soul; thus bestowing the crown of martyrdom upon those who had not yet come to the use of reason.

I adore the equity of your judgements, manifested in all your works: you exalted the pure and humble to your everlasting glory; but cast down into hell, there to be confounded for ever, Herod and the partners in his guilt.

I earnestly implore you, O most pure Jesus, to give me, of your mercy, grace to follow, in heart and life, the innocence, and the humility of those little ones; so that, laying aside all rancour and arrogance, I may henceforth show myself among my brethren, more gentle, more pure, more lowly, more patient, and more cheerful. May no weakness of the flesh defile me; but by a thorough mortification of my faults may I be kept pure and without offence. **Amen**.

Jesus in the Temple

Luke 2: 41-50

I bless you, and give thanks to you, O Lord Jesus Christ, pattern of humility and mighty teacher of eternal truth, for the example of your stupendous humility, and for the light of your hidden wisdom, shown forth to men, at your going up to Jerusalem with your parents for the Feast; you offered for us to God the Father sacrifices of holy prayer and praise, and sat humbly, as a boy of twelve, in the midst of the doctors, hearing them and discreetly asking them questions, fixing upon yourself the attention of all present.

I praise you, and I magnify with the deepest devotion your holy name, for the reverent obedience which you showed to your parents who for a long time sought you, and at length found you; in that you, the King of heaven, renouncing straightway your own will, humbly submitted to their authority; and, although they did not understand the saying which you spoke unto them, yet you went down with them from Jerusalem to Nazareth, and there showed yourself as the most obedient of sons to the best of mothers.

O most sweet Jesus, most loving of sons, mirror of holiness and of every virtue, teach me, I pray you, to subdue the perverseness of my will; cheerfully to bow to the advice of my elders; devoutly to visit the temple of God; diligently to hear and declare your Word; to venerate the doctors of the Church; to obey my superiors cheerfully; and to serve you joyfully all the days of my life, submitting myself in all things to your holy will. **Amen**.

The hidden life of Jesus

Luke 2: 51-52

I bless you, and give thanks to you, O Lord Jesus Christ, for the surpassing holiness of that hidden life, which for so long a time you pursued in the house of your parents at Nazareth. You dwelt with them in great poverty, lowliness, and subjection, from your twelfth to your thirtieth year.

I most heartily praise and magnify you for your condescension in veiling your majesty from those among whom you dwelt, in that you deigned to be called, and to be believed to be, the son of a carpenter; and openly did nothing from which your Godhead might be known.

O the humility of Christ! O my God, how you confound my foolish self-conceit; how, by your bright example, you bid me avoid all outward show, turn aside from men of the world, choose to lead a secluded life, seek to be known to God alone, make the salvation of my soul my chief aim, not put myself forward, even for the sake of edification; but rather strive to lay diligently to heart the word of life, until such time as the heavenly call shall come to bring forth fruit!

Help me, sweet Jesus, gracious Master, to understand, by diligent meditation upon it, the character of your hidden life; to dedicate my own inner self to you; ever to love a humble and secluded life, taking no heed of the things of this world; but cherishing rather, as the objects of my love, the things which concern you and my home in heaven; and, in the secret closet of my heart, to treasure up the story of your most holy life and conversation. **Amen**.

Jesus is baptized

Matt. 3; Luke 3: 1-22; John 1: 19-34

 bless you, and give thanks to you, O Lord Jesus Christ, fountain of goodness, and source of every virtue, for humbly receiving holy baptism; for fulfilling all righteousness; for voluntarily putting yourself into the hands of your forerunner, by whom you agreed to be baptized in the river Jordan; thus consecrating for us the waters of baptism, and by your example showing to all those who come to that holy rite, be they of high or be they of low estate, how needful it is for them humbly to receive the sacrament of new birth unto salvation, if they would find a place at last in the mansions of your heavenly kingdom.

In your baptism we too have been washed; that sanctification was for our profit, not for yours; for you were without any spot of sin.

I praise and magnify you, O divine and adorable Head, before which even the angelic spirits veil their faces, for most humbly bowing yourself, for going down into the Jordan, and for receiving its waters upon yourself, for the washing away of our sins.

I bless you and glorify your holy name, for your revelation of heavenly mysteries; for the presence of the most Holy Trinity manifestly shown forth; for the way of entrance into everlasting life opened out to us; for your wondrous enlightenment of John the Baptist, your blessed forerunner; for his humble answer to those who questioned him; and for his ready obedience to your word.

O my Jesus, most highly exalted King, how greatly you abased yourself this day for me, the vilest of sinners; what stores of divine grace have you opened to me by this condescension! Look upon me, and mercifully forgive all the sins, of which, openly and secretly, I have in so many ways been guilty.

I pray to be baptized by you with the Holy Spirit and with fire; for I have in many things offended your goodness. Wash me thoroughly from my wickedness, and cleanse me from my sin. No one is free from the stain of sin, not even the infant of a day; in all the world no one is pure but you alone, the Purifier; you alone, the Sanctifier, are holy, who, according to the multitude of your mercies, have power to forgive men their sins.

Be gracious unto me, I beseech you, O Lord, and let my soul live; nor remember my former sins, but renew my youth like the eagle's. Forgive what is past; cause me to take heed to my ways in the days that are to come: grant me ever fresh supplies of grace, so that at last I may be found meet to dwell with you in the kingdom of everlasting glory. **Amen**.

Jesus performs miracles

Mark 1: 27-28; 32-34

bless you, and give thanks to you, O Lord Jesus Christ, power of God, and wisdom of the Father, for the glorious signs and mighty wonders, by which you shed forth upon the world your glorious Light, and made known your truth even to those sitting in darkness; openly showing yourself, by infallible proofs and incontestable miracles, to be the Christ, the Son of the living God, who had come into the world to be the Saviour of mankind.

I praise and glorify you for your boundless love, in that you showed yourself to all men so kind and so good, that not only the poor and the sick, but even the vilest sinners, were not afraid to come to you; and were allowed freely to speak to you, and to touch you.

Blessed be those eyes, shining more brightly than the sun, which turned, full of pity, upon the crowds who came to you, to whom you were so gracious and so compassionate that you would not send them away fasting to their homes; but rather did, not once only but twice, by working a great miracle, more than satisfy many thousands with a few loaves, and some small fishes.

Blessed be those adorable hands, which you freely laid upon so many sick folk; healing at once, by the touch of your most sacred body, all their diseases and infirmities.

Blessed be those all-beautiful feet, so often wearied, and besmeared with dust, for the salvation of souls, which you used when going to and fro upon the earth, sowing plenteously the word of life, proclaiming it to all men, now upon the mountain side, now upon the open plain – working, moreover, in proof of your holy doctrine, frequent miracles, causing men sick of the palsy to go upon their feet, giving sight to the blind, cleansing lepers, casting out devils, and, by the power of God, bringing back the dead to life.

O adorable Jesus, light of the world, salvation of your people Israel, our life, our light, and our glory, turn your eye of mercy, I beseech you, upon my infirmity, and drive out from my heart every evil lust: give sight to the eyes of my soul, that I may see the heavenly light: open the ears of my understanding that I may hear, O my God, what you have to say to me: raise me from my bed of sloth, that I may go on from strength to strength: direct my feet in the path of your commandments, and give power to my withered hands for earnest work in your service: cleanse me from the leprosy of the flesh; cure me of the madness of anger; subdue in me the swelling of pride; pluck out from my heart the sting of envy; keep me from excess in eating; drive far from me the plague of covetousness, and crush within me all my impure desires.

These most grievous afflictions of an ailing soul, these secret impulses of the devil and his angels, can be healed by you alone, O Lord; can be cast out by no other means than by your resistless Word. None can heal these spiritual wounds, none can work wonders of holiness in the inner life, but you alone, O Almighty God, who speak and it is done, who command and straightway your order takes effect. Say therefore, I beseech you, to my soul: 'Be thou clean,' and forthwith it shall be cleansed: say to the unclean spirit which so often tempts me: 'Go out of the man, and enter no more into him': say to my soul, whenever trouble comes upon me, 'Fear not, I am Thy salvation': speak but one word only, and my soul shall be healed. **Amen**.

CHRISTMAS 14

Jesus provides an example

Matt. 11: 25-30

 Lord Jesus Christ, pattern of holiness, model of all perfection, flower of virtue, savour of life, mirror of patience, I bless you for your beauteous life, for your surpassing gentleness, and for the faultless example which you openly set to your disciples, and to all the people of Israel; thus sweetly drawing to the love of you the souls of the lowly in heart, moving to repentance, by the gentle tenderness of your words, the hard hearts of sinners, and matchlessly instructing the learned, by your every act, and by every word of your teaching.

I praise and glorify you for all the bodily wants and hardships suffered by you whilst in the world. Having taken upon yourself our mortal nature, from the hour of your birth to the hour of your death upon the Cross, you vouchsafed to undergo for us, creatures of earth and appointed to death, hunger often and thirst, cold and heat, toil and weariness, sadness and anxiety; and you endured all this with perfect mildness and resignation of heart.

130

I praise and glorify you for the malicious snares so often set for you; for the many and grievous persecutions and shameful blasphemies so often inflicted upon you by the scribes and Pharisees; and for the monstrous ingratitude, and the odious slanders, with which your chosen people repaid you for the innumerable benefits and the mighty wonders, which you so gloriously worked among them.

I praise and magnify you for the unspeakable travail of your soul for the conversion and salvation of mankind; for the many long watches of the night which you passed in prayer for us; for the groans and for the tears, which you poured forth in pity for us; for your joy and satisfaction over those who were converted to the faith; for your sublime thanksgivings, and the upliftings of your soul; and for the works – so many and so marvellous – wrought by you, to the praise and glory of your heavenly Father.

O most adorable Jesus, brightest mirror of a holy life, grant, I beseech you, to me, your unworthy servant (whose life has hitherto been most grievously at variance with your holy will), so to meditate upon your most sweet and perfect example, that I may be led to fashion all my actions and behaviour in accordance with it; that I may learn from it to be meek and lowly in heart; to be moderate in my taking of food; simple in my dress; modest in my bearing; not hurried in my walking; calm in my mind; not an idle talker; prudent in my actions; guarded both as to my outward and my inward life; watchful in prayer; devout in meditation; patient under correction; prompt in obedience; easy to be led in every good way; not slow, not careless, not sullen, not restless, not inconstant, not noisy; but kind, cheerful, affable, and unassuming.   **Amen**.